THE HID

BY KAMILAH HAYWOOD

KYAPUBLISHING.COM

Management: Amanda Godda

F-You Project: Tara Muldoon

Graphic Designer: Sui Young

Photographer: Symone Sparks

Model: Deanna Cassis

All rights reserved. No part of this publication may be reproduced, stored in a retrieval system, or transmitted, in any form or by any means, without the prior written permission of the publisher.

This book is a work of fiction. Names, characters, places, and incidents are either products of the author's imagination or are used fictitiously. Any resemblance to actual events, locales, or persons (living or dead) is entirely coincidental.

Haywood, Kamilah, 1980-

ISBN-13: 978-0-9879195-5-7

www.KyaPublishing.com

© 2021 by Kya Publishing

*"Universal law—cause and effect, equated with karma—
is when the slave turns into the slave master, and when
the predator becomes the prey."*

K. Haywood

To all the lost souls on the hidden track whose stories inspire many to change. Thank you.

RWAY4Life

Lucky 11

This book is dedicated to Grandpa, Mama, Grandma, Aunty Sonia, Aunty Nicola, Cuzzo Tasha, Klay, Peter, Chady Blkz, Quest, Doughboy, FattKidd, Hubba, Corey, Saby, Rex, & Scottie. This one's for all y'all.

For anyone who believed in and supported me along this journey—especially my Mom: this is dedicated to you.

To all the BIPOC and Women that were a part of this project: thank you!

This book is also dedicated to the Freeland of North Preston: the first Black Indigenous community that escaped their slave masters, built a community out of nothing, and turned it into something...by any means necessary!

To the Indigenous children who died at the hands of this evil, corrupt, dark, broken system: this book is also dedicated to you. Y'all are the TRUE heroes. BIG UP.

#JUSTICEFOREGIS
#JUSTICEFORD'ANDRE
#JUSTICEFORJAMAL
#JUSTICEFOREJAZ

...AND THE OTHERS WE HAVE LOST TO THIS SYSTEM!

CHAPTER 1: TOUCH

Present

There are times I would get lost in the cracks of the ceilings. I mean, I could envision a life that seemed so close to reality...yet so distant. I would search in the ceiling for a face or an image of anything to take me away—something that could take me out of my present reality.

    I could use the ceiling as a mirror of my own reflection; it was as if my eyes would create an illusion to keep me contained. I would lose all feelings of anything that felt human. This became a normal ritual. It was as if some part of me knew how to take over my body or my mind...or maybe it was just the drugs. Maybe it was the constant binges I would go on to cope, staying up for days to get high. Going up on a Tuesday and yet still up when the next Tuesday came around...but by Wednesday I was done. The crash came heavy, and I became sloppy. My body would totally collapse on day seven. The day of rest.

    Maybe it was his words on repeat: "I love you, baby."

    His touch—that I was feeling deep down inside—gave me the strength to keep going, yet the more I continued, the more I felt like I was at the same spot...not moving anywhere.

    The more money that came in, the more money that went out, but the house with the white picket fence with our two babies was still there waiting for us. Our dream. I would marry him and be his Queen forever. Our love was that deep.

    His words sent chills down my spine; I could get lost in his smile. He was so different from any man I had ever met. My King. He would always be just that: my King.

"OOOOH yeah! Ooooh fuckin' yeah. Fuck baby! Your pussy's so tight. Yeah baby, right there! Right fuckin' there. I'm gonna cum!" he said as his body jerked faster and faster, releasing his load inside me.

He was trying to stay inside (giving me the saddest case of fuck lap dance), but his thirty minutes was up. I pushed his fat, hairy, white, sweaty body off me as I woke up from the dream world in the ceiling where I was visualizing getting lost in forever...and not coming back.

The cheap hotel we were in was a mess. Cigarette ashtrays were full, garbage was overflowing, and the washroom was a disaster from the party last night. I had been up for three days and needed to sleep.

Cleaning was not always a number one priority on my list when it was a busy night, however. I mean, I had more money to be made. Five hundred more to be exact, and then I could rest and move locations.

I hated when Ice booked us in shitty hotels. Yes, it was cheaper, but some of my clientele wouldn't even come to those hotels because they knew it was a hot spot. They knew every new bitch on the block gets put up in spots like these to start out, but little did these new bitches know there was a lifestyle and a history that went along with the game: the illusion you're selling to these tricks.

Ice only put me here tonight as punishment, and because I didn't make enough money last night because I got too high. He was punishing me and had not called me all day—not even to check in. He was just running the work phone and sending clients over while texting me in the process, so I was ready.

I knew the drill: if I had not made twenty-five hundred by night's end, it would be a problem. We had a vision, and I had to do my part to make it work just like he did.

"This was a fuckin' suite, my ass!" I mumbled to myself.

"What did you say pumpkin?" He approached the washroom in his white boxers, carrying the condom he removed from his red, shriveled up penis hanging out his boxer briefs.

He had brown stained teeth from too much coffee and cigarettes but could not close his mouth for the life of him. He was trying to hold on to the little brown strands of hair poking out the sides of his head.

"Nothing. I'm just getting a bath ready."

"Bath? I thought we had another round?"

"That's another five hundred."

"You're breaking my balls!"

"Go home to your wife, Johnny! I'm sure she has a nice Italian feast waiting for you."

"You don't play nice! When can I see you again?" he said, walking away to grab his clothes off the hotel chair.

"You know the drill, Johnny!"

Johnny reached in his pocket and grabbed a stack of cash. He grabbed three crisp, brown hundred-dollar bills.

"Here's a tip for always being you! Buy yourself something nice, and here is a treat I brought you 'cause I know you like it…but you really need to lay off it." Johnny passed me the money and about a gram of cocaine. I could not help but smile—he always had the best cocaine. The shit Ice picked up always got too much cut, making my high get fucked up and paranoid.

"See you later, Johnny!"

"Ok, Baby Cakes!"

The Mississauga strip of hotels were all selling pussy for a cheap price—it was no wonder my clients didn't want to come here. At nighttime, it was infested with cops, and there is always at least one John trying to call his wife saying he got locked up for buying pussy.

It was not long before I was able to soak my tired body in the bathtub. I set up everything nice: champagne and cocaine, my breakfast of champions. A little C & C time is always needed after a long day of work. I mean, how else was a girl supposed to handle this life?

I had so much acting to do, to feed these hopeless, pathetic men a dream they could never have. Some just wanted the pussy, but others wanted a wife with my looks to take care of. The pussy was the control. Pussy had the power to control many things, and weak-minded men were one of them.

The soothing hot water on my skin (with Epsom salt to top it off) was to die for. It always kept my body intact. I grabbed my glass of rose Moet to soothe me—it went down smooth, fulfilling every taste bud in my mouth. I had my mirror set up by the bathtub with a crisp one-hundred-dollar bill, and I opened the bag of bleach, white, and cocaine. I made a huge thick line as it had been a while (or it seemed like it) since my last bump. All I knew was I sure needed a wake up to pull me back together.

The tingly feeling in the back of my throat mixed with the taste of pure cocaine. I needed more. I started to hear all kinds of noises and I knew it was my paranoia. I could hear Ice's voice coming closer and closer—this always happened after days of staying up. My mind would play tricks on me and sometimes my vision.

I dipped my head down in the bathtub. The water always had a way of calming things. It's funny we forget water is a healer. My Pisces ass always remembered, because I loved the water...the warmth of the water massaging my body. A new fresh start to a day's work. I had five hundred more to make.

I sunk my body into the bathtub, and my eyes started to close. It must have been the champagne. I sat up and opened the bag of cocaine to make another line to pick me up.

Someone began knocking at the door. The light knocks eventually started to get louder and faster, so I quickly jumped out of the tub, grabbing a white hotel towel to cover my body. The knocks continued, louder.

"I'M COMING!" I said, rushing to open the door. The knocks continued when I flung the door open as fast as I could to see who it was. Before I could even look, Ice pushed his way in the door. His six foot two muscular, caramel body was no match to my five foot five slim, white—but tanned—body.

Ice was always dressed in the best clothes, and today Versace was his selection. He had on that Versace sweater Biggie (the famous rapper) used to wear before he passed, and the same vintage Versace glasses. He had on dark denim jeans with mustard, classic Timberland boots. He looked good, as always. Good enough to eat.

"YOU GIRL! You didn't hear the knock?" he said, pacing from side to side.

He took his sunglasses off after barging in, and I knew he was angry because of his tone. His eyes investigated each corner of the room. He made his way to the bathtub, grabbed the Moet bottle, the cocaine bag, and the one-hundred-dollar bill.

"Why are you not answering my texts?" he said, holding up the bottle and a bag of cocaine. I did not respond. I just looked at him.

"Now cat got your fuckin' tongue, eh You Girl!" he said. The anger on his face! I put my head down. The beautiful, brown-skinned man with his pretty boy smile was nowhere to be found. He was a monster now...one I feared meeting. This was not my baby Ice. I was not sure who this was, but I hated him.

"Now you can't talk? Get on your knees now, You Girl! You were already under punishment, but now you're fucked up! Don't answer my calls, fuckin' up business last night cause you're high? Today the same shit? I already told you 'bout this! Crawl over here to your Daddy," he said. I was in fear of the punishment. I mean, two days in a row that I fucked up meant double punishment.

Before I could even begin crawling, he smashed the bottle over my head, causing me to see stars as I fell to the ground.

"YOU WANNA PLAY AROUND WITH OUR DREAM? OUR KIDS' FUTURE?" he said, raising his voice. My head was numb, and I started to feel blood running down my face when Ice started kicking me repeatedly in my stomach.

"You goin' learn today! I paid for that bleach blonde weave you got on! I can rip it out!" I just laid there, taking this beating. It was not the first and would not be the last.

Ice grabbed my long, blonde, six-hundred-dollar human hair weave. He was pulling my head all over the floor, while slapping me on my ass...hard. I was naked with my towel on the floor, and blood down my face.
"Look what you make me do, baby? Look what you make me do?" He unstrapped his belt and started lashing me with it. I couldn't hold the pain any longer. I started to cry uncontrollably. Ice paused the lash whipping.

"You goin' listen to Daddy now eh, You Girl?" He unbuckled his pants and pulled down his jeans and Tommy Hilfiger boxers. "What do you want right now, baby? You want your Daddy?"

"YES!"

"Say it again!"

"YES DADDY!" My body was throbbing with pain. My face was full of blood. I tried to hold back my tears but Ice forcibly rammed his penis inside me so hard it made me cry even worse in agony. He fucked hard and fast.

"Who's your Daddy? Who's your Daddy?" he repeated until his body started spazzing uncontrollably. I hated when he did not wear a condom. The amount of abortions I had to get because of Ice.

"Why do you make me get angry? All you have to do is listen like a good girl! Clean yourself up! Bob is coming to pick us up in an hour to bring us to the Trump hotel downtown. He needs you for a couple days. He's gonna take you shopping and give you five grand."

I did not say a word. I just did as I was told—it was the only way to make him happy. His happiness was what made me feel worthy enough to keep going.

CHAPTER 2: RETRO

8 Years Ago (2011)

The down home had its way with my soul. I mean, I always loved the person I was in the country. My Mama always said I would be a star. The way I would sing around the house, waving my blonde curly locks all over the place, and dancing. I would envision myself as a celebrity or auditioning for Canada's Got Talent. I would have loved to audition for Canadian Idol but I was too young. The age limit was sixteen, and I had just turned thirteen. I knew I would make it in that competition...or at least that's what I convinced myself of.

Auditions were coming in two weeks, and finally they decided to expand and bring it to Nova Scotia, my hometown. Some say Nova Scotia is New Scotland, but I don't know much about that.

Mama said one day she would take me to see the real Scotland. She always told me the Scottish discovered

Nova Scotia and that's where my ancestors were from. My Daddy always argued with Mama, telling her his people were the founders of Canada until the Europeans stole it from them. My Daddy was mixed with both Native Indian and African Canadian. He was a dark chocolate-skinned, curly, long-haired man with a tall and muscular shape. His father was Mi'kmaq Indigenous Indian, and his mother was an African American settler. His mother died at an early age from cancer; my great grandmother, Daddy, said she was a slave that escaped from Alabama in the United States.

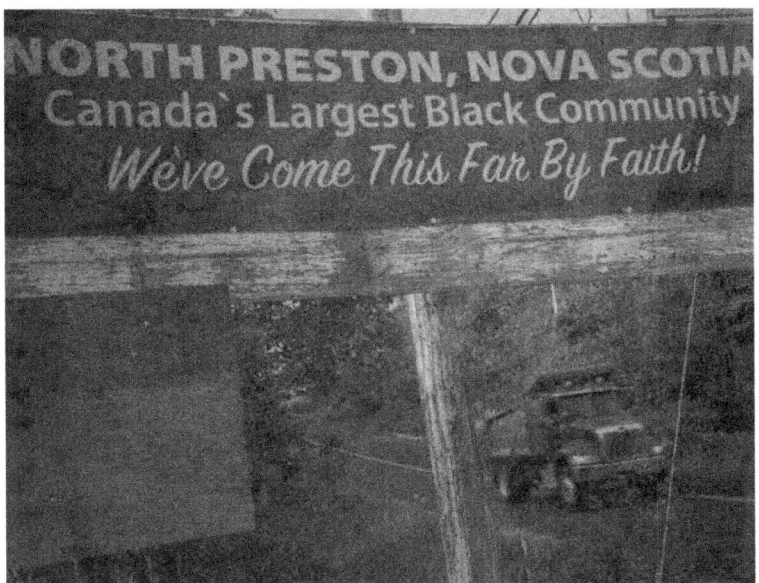

He told me stories of his tribe (my Granpy and Great Grandpa's tribe) the Mi'kmaq. He said they were the founders of Nova Scotia, P.E.I., and Newfoundland—the Atlantic east coast of Canada.

He recalled stories of the invasion of the Europeans and how they destroyed the land and the water by taking resources for greed, motivated by corruption. My Daddy's stories seemed more factual than Mama's, but where did that leave me? I had blonde, light, brown, curly hair, and light caramel skin with green eyes that turned hazel depending on my mood (Mama said). I was slim and taller than most girls in my grade, with bigger feet as well. Granpy said I got that from Daddy.

I always felt pulled between two worlds and that I had to explain myself about which side I would choose. Sometimes, I was left feeling alone.

I was mixed: Scottish, African, and Native Indian, Canadian. I was lucky, like my Granpy told me. I had the best of many worlds, and I would discover myself along with my purpose in between those worlds...creating a balance most never knew existed. We all had a purpose, he would tell me when I was younger, but I still had yet to figure out what he meant by that.

I was left alone a lot with Granpy because Daddy was always at work with his trucking business to support our family, and my Mama was busy at the bingo hall trying to win back the money my dad gave her for bills that she never used wisely. Mama always had a lying excuse to Daddy, but Daddy would still give her more and more money anyway.

Being alone with Granpy was an experience within itself. Granpy taught me things about life that only a wise elder from his tribe would know, being passed on to him as a young boy. Sometimes I would get really mesmerized at the experiences he faced—he walked with the greats of this Canadian land, and they taught him many things you would never learn in school. Granpy said the schools were a form of control meant to enslave the young mind and the spirit, leaving the body dead walking. He expressed terrifying stories of the schools they were forced to attend; he said they tried to make the children forget their way of living to adjust to the white man's new world order.

I always wondered what the spirit was because he kept telling me my spirit would be one of many experiences and lives. He said my spirit would change the world. I just laughed and listened, but something inside of me knew he was right. It was like I had heard these stories before.

Granpy was a medium-built sized man with darker brown skin—his hair was long to the middle of his back. He pulled his black, curly, thick locks back in a ponytail and always wore a red bandana around his head. He loved to dance and was always howling some type of song for me to dance to...like a wolf. Granpy was the best person in my life.

One morning when Mama was off at bingo for some big jackpot that everyone in town was talking about in North Preston, I had just come inside for a drink, and from playing with my friends, when the phone rang.

I quickly ran through the kitchen, almost dropping my cup, and I could hear Mama screaming at me for always breaking her shit. For someone who idolized her possessions, she sure had a way of making others feel small when they damaged her belongings. Daddy was the complete opposite. He showed so much love and made sure to clarify to Mama that they were just things. Mama would get right mad, as if Daddy had taken her life away. My Daddy was all about love and heart...just like Granpy.

I answered the phone, and it was Daddy.

"Hey baby girl, where's your Mama?" I could hear the background noise of the traffic Daddy was in.

"Hi Daddy! Where are you?" I asked.

"I'm in Chicago dropping a load. Your Mama home?"

"No Daddy!"

"She's not answering her cell phone, so I guess we know what that means. Damn woman can't keep a dollar in her pocket with all that gambling." I did not respond, and Daddy must have felt my vibe in the silence because he quickly changed his tone and the topic.

"I'll be home later on tonight, and I'm gonna send Granpy over 'til your Mama gets home." Daddy always smiled at me with deep eyes that connected to his soul. I could feel his love.

"Ok Daddy. See you soon."

"Love you, baby girl!"

"Love you too, Daddy!" I sat quietly, waiting to see if Daddy would say anything else, but he hung up before I could tell him I wanted him to come to the auditions.

"Right Christ, chile! I don't know how many times I gotta tell you to clean up before your Daddy gets home!" Mama said, rushing through the door with some takeout she brought home. Mama always brought takeout home if she won at bingo, or if she was at bingo all day and did not make dinner before Daddy came home. Mama always had a way of ruining a good day. As soon as she walked in the door, I turned into a house maid. I had so many chores, I wondered what Mama's role was.

Mama was a big dictator and controller, and Daddy allowed her to be that way. Don't get me wrong: Daddy has faults of his own. He was a big drinker—something Mama hated—and she would use that against him to control him. I hated to watch Mama break Daddy down, but Daddy allowed it because he loved her so much, he would give her whatever she asked for, for her love in return. If he could do it, he would. Mama never seemed to listen or care about anyone's feelings but her own.

A part of me hated her and hated her even more as part of her became a part of my own reflection. Mama always pushed me away in every way she could except when she needed me to do something for her, or hide the mess she made spending all Daddy's money at bingo...and like a good, obedient child (I was at the time)...I did anything Mama asked of me I did because all I wanted was for her to see and accept me for who I was: her child longing for love. Love that only came from Daddy when he was around and present, or from Granpy whose love was unconditional.

Daddy had allowed Mama to be the selfish woman she was. She binged at bingo, and each day it became worse, the more she was consumed in her gambling addiction.

The day finally came for the singing competition, and I was up early, preparing myself.

Our house was a small house in the North Preston community—it looked more like a shack, if you asked me. North Preston was a segregated Indigenous Black community. Mama hated us living there, but that's where most of Daddy's family originated from. Granpy said they were the only Indigenous Black people given land from slavery over two hundred years ago. There was always an argument about if Granpy's tribe was Indian or Black. They looked like both, but that's a whole other story.

North Preston was an isolated community full of folks who originated from the south in the United States, after migrating after slavery, and the Maroons from Jamaica. Daddy said most of the Jamaicans left a long time ago, however.

Mama hated living in an all-Black community at first, but was well adjusted once she found friends at church that later became her bingo company.

Mama and Daddy met on one of Daddy's local truck runs in Halifax. Mama was working at a bar when Daddy walked in, and it was love at first sight. They always laugh when they tell the story, but a lot of people never liked them together because they were an interracial couple. It was never accepted, but they did it anyway.

Mama was a diva and acted like the world owed her something...and when she didn't get her own way, she was a bitch, and she made us suffer in her misery until she was ready to let it go. Parts of me hated her, and maybe it was because she instilled fear in me. I had to act like I liked her, but deep down I loved her more than I loved anyone...if only she would see me for who I was. If only she would love me for the person I was, instead of who she thought I should be.

I remember Granpy saying that people love you to the best of their abilities. He explained the three types of lovers: those that loved you by buying gifts as a token of their love, those that loved you by expressing it with their thoughts and feelings, and he then explained a love from those who never said a word but showed you (in their actions and unconditional love) that they accepted everything about you, no matter what form or package it came in.

Mama was the first type, and Daddy was the third. Granpy was the third type, and that left me. I was not sure what type of lover I was, but I knew it was nothing like Mama's.

•

Granpy rushed me through the Canada's Got Talent audition doors to a packed group of contestants lining up and waiting for their chance to make it. We drove to downtown Halifax where the competition was taking place; the journey was the worst drive of my life. I felt like I had to vomit every time Granpy accelerated on the gas.

The nerves in my belly were out of this world! I was nauseous as I waited for my turn to register for a chance to audition. I watched many of the contestants performing and practicing their auditions. There were all types: singers, dancers, magicians, jugglers, comedians, contortionists, and trapeze artists...just to name a few. I watched as disappointed contestants left the audition room, crying as they did not make the first round.

Granpy kept rubbing my back and asking if I was ok. I was not ok.

"Listen Lily. I call you Lily because just like you, the flower is pure, innocent, and beautiful...plus you also grew from the bulb to a flower, just like one. When you feel uncomfortable in your own skin, that means you are doing something right. Your comfort zone is easy, but when you're not in your comfort zone and keep trying, that is what separates you from the rest. That is how you find your path, and who you are deep down inside. You can do this. Your voice is like magic to my soul! Show these judges your magic," he said.

It was the sweetest thing Granpy ever said to me, but it also made me feel strength...like I could do this. The confidence came from an unknown existence and when it was my turn, I knew I would not fail.

As I walked towards the audition room after they called my number, I watched all the smiles (and also looks of fear) upon entering the room. I suddenly felt this wave of emotion throttle through my body. My nerves were vibrating all through my skin, reacting in goosebumps. I started to fix the beige, flower dress Granpy bought me for the auditions. The dress fell upon my figure, accenting the shape of my body. Granpy kept smiling at me, telling me I was going to be a star.

I entered the audition room, waving Granpy goodbye. He blew a kiss at me, and I caught it. The three judges sitting at the table were two males and a female. They immediately smiled when they noticed what they had just witnessed.

"Aww that is so cute," the lady spoke. She was beautiful with her brown curly locks, straight white teeth, and big blue gorgeous eyes. She was a rare beauty—nothing like what I had ever witnessed in Nova Scotia. Her style was to die for. She looked like a model from some fashion magazine Mama used to read, wishing she had those women's lives. Mama swore she was supposed to be in some foreign place living the glamorous life.

"Hi! What are you performing today?" The first male spoke. He was white, with long dirty blonde hair, and dressed in all black with dark black sunglasses. He did not look at me at all when he spoke…not that I could have observed with his sunglasses on anyway.

My nerves got a bit shot, but I did not flinch or show that I was nervous.

"Amy Winehouse, Unholy War," I said, looking away from all the judges who were now staring at me.

"Ok! Let's hear it!" the female judge said.

"That's some big shoes to fill," the male judge with sunglasses spoke as he slowly began to remove them. His big dark brown eyes connected with mine, but I did not let him intimidate me. I knew what I was yearning to release from my soul. I knew what I had come here for.

I entered my front door to notice Mama sitting on the couch, smoking a cigarette—a cigarette she would not be smoking if Daddy or Granpy were in the house.

I had my Canada's Got Talent audition acceptance slip in my hand, and I made it through to the next round. I smiled at Mama when I walked through the door, but she did not look at me. Instead, she continued smoking her cigarette in a daydream. Soulless. Her eyes were dark; her body was limp.

"MAMA! You ok?" She was silent and continued in a daydream. I hated days like this. I hated Mama like this. "Mama, you ok?" I dropped my yellow slip on the floor and went towards Mama to hug her as always. Mama dropped her cigarette on the floor and it hit the brown old carpet we had in our living room. Her head fell back and her eyes rolled back in her head. Her body went limp in the brown, old, three-seat, suede couch my Daddy had taken from my Granpy a while back. It was my Grandma's couch before she passed away, and Granpy said he had no reason to keep it now that she was gone.

I wrapped my arms around her lifeless body as her eyes became darker. The Mama I once knew was distant from this physical body that sat before me. I felt the warmth of her body, but her soul was gone. My Mama was gone.

•

I froze in her arms, but my soul screamed until the cries came out of my mouth and I sobbed.

"MAMA!"

A piece of me died that day with her. A piece of me I will never get back. Everything went dark and what was once normal became foreign. My heart stopped, and it felt like I was in a dream.

I stayed in Mama's arms until Granpy found me the next day.

"Baby girl! You want some breakfast? I was thinkin' we could..." Granpy ran towards me leaving the front door wide open and dropped his belongings on the floor. He stood looking at Mama and me for a moment.

Mama's body began to get cold. Her spirit (as Granpy would say) was free and in a higher vibration.

Granpy tried to pull me off of Mama, but I had a hard time releasing my grip from her. I knew this was the last time she would be in my arms like this again. It was the only time I could remember that I could hold, love, and cuddle her without her pushing me away. I put all the love I had for her in that moment because I knew I would never have the chance.

"Come," Granpy said in a whisper. It was the early morning—brisk of dawn—I could barely see any light in the house. I saw a tiny little shimmering teardrop fall down Granpy's face, and I burst into a huge scream. That was the first time I'd ever witnessed a grown man cry before.

"Shhh! It goin..." Granpy couldn't get the words out. His voice was muffled, and the pitch of his deep raspy voice went so high for a moment...that he just stopped speaking. The bitter silence filled our small, dark living room. I could barely see, as the tears continued to roll down my face. My chest felt like it wanted to cave in.

Granpy carried me in my room and gently laid me down on my bed. He tried to let go, but I could not let go, so Granpy laid with me all night. He stroked my hair gently until I fell asleep. I could still feel Mama's presence around...it was so weird. I could still hear her voice. I kept wondering: where Mama is now?

CHAPTER 3: DOWN HOME

We cremated Mama, as she always said to do, and her ashes were to be spread in the mountains of Scotland. She advised Daddy to take her there.

The thought of Mama gone was like a knife in my chest.

The silence that remained in our home was morbid, and Daddy sat in the place where Mama died and drank. He slept, ate, and did not bathe for days. I watched as the aromas of beer bottles and dirty body odour began to stink up the entire house.

It was not until Granpy came to check on us that he cleaned up Daddy and his mess. Daddy was laying in his vomit on the floor, lifeless, when Granpy slapped him up out of his vomit. He picked up Daddy's drunk, lifeless body, and dragged him to the washroom. He pushed Daddy in the small, brown, bathtub that had not been washed since before Mama died.

Granpy came up behind me and flicked my ear gently, smiling. I jumped up, but when I looked at him, his eyes were light grey. I blinked my eyes and looked at Granpy again, but his eyes flashed to dark brown, his normal colour.

"Granpy, there's somethin…"

"Shhhhhhhh! My young eagle, one day I will show you, but for now be still." I listened to Granpy no matter what—his words had a deep connection to my soul. Like no matter what, he would always know what was right, and I was just listening while I received his guidance.

"I am going to stay here for a while, until everything is right. Right?" he said.

"Yes, right!"

"One day you will realize that everything in your life is exactly how it is supposed to be. You must not challenge or go against the flow of the universe."

"Granpy, is Daddy going to be ok?"

"Yes! He is a warrior just like you, and no matter what comes in his path, he will always conquer it! Sometimes you have to walk in the dark to find the warrior within you."

"What warrior?"

"When the student is ready, the master will appear."

"What master? Granpy, what are you talking about?"

"Sing for me, my young eagle. When you sing…the world stops! My Lily!"

"I don't want to sing anymore. Forget singing!" I got up off the couch and walked towards my bedroom, but Granpy pulled my arm.

"My young eagle. You have a gift; you must use it!"

"LEAVE ME!" I ran to my room and slammed the door—plopped myself down on my bed.

I could hear Granpy's footsteps coming to the door, but after he heard no response, he walked away. My emotions were a mess from Mama dying to Daddy being a mess because of Mama's death. I mean, where did that leave me? What was I supposed to do or how could I explain the emotional load that just sat on my chest?

The pain was heavy, and I kept trying to stuff it down inside to get to the next moment. The moments became a blur. The silence became loud. The darkness became darker. My body was exhausted, and my thoughts became a chattering voice, slandering everything that got close to me…or seemed to.

I could hear Mama now: "You worthless chil', sittin' around crying over spilt milk! I could never cry, after all that's been done to me! Cry for fuckin' what? Your Daddy cries enough for the both of us, and now you want to be like him? Fuckin' useless!"

The tears would not come. The lump in my throat...I swallowed, tasting the salty taste of my silva. I laid in my bed staring at the ceiling, wondering if I would ever get to hold Mama's hand again. No matter what she did to me, she would always be my Mama. The only Mama I would ever know.

It took a while for me to be able to return back to school, but Granpy knew it was time because he noticed I was falling further into depression and social isolation. He spoke with Daddy—who was on the road back to work—and told him he was going to get me to return to school the following Monday.

I loved my school. It was the oldest all Black school in Canada, and the only school in North Preston.

My teacher Mrs. Jenkin always corrected me saying Indigenous, but I didn't really understand the meaning of Indigenous. If you were Black or had some Black in you and lived in our community, that's why you were attending this school.

Mama protested me going, but the ladies in our community convinced her it would be good for me to learn about Daddy's history and a part of my own history as well.

Nelson Whynder Elementary School was not a large school; there were only five teachers that each had full classrooms. Mama always complained there were not enough students or teachers to learn properly. She would always complain about autistic and behavioural students in the same classes with 'normal' students. My Daddy would always correct her that kids are kids, but Mama was too ignorant to care. Mama felt because the school was primarily African Canadian, that the education system was not the best. She felt we were getting pushed aside and taught the basics to survive to stay in North Preston.

Daddy always told Mama I was learning about my history and at the same time I could get to go to the dentist: now that I loved it. Since I started this school, I had been going to the dentist there. Most of the children in the North Preston community came to this school to go to the dentist. Daddy told Mama if she had a job, that she would have to take me to the dentist somewhere else, but because I came to Nelson Whynder, I could get the best of both worlds before school was finished. Mama was always about a deal (or something being offered) for her to agree. In the end, she approved because of free dental and not education.

During Christmas, the school organized for volunteers to come and put on a Christmas dinner for us. We would get gifts and some good Christmas dinner all for free.

After the first dinner, Mama never mentioned she did not want me going to school again. She was happy to get the help from the community for me.

"Welcome BACKKKKK!" My whole classroom screamed as I entered the classroom. I wanted to turn around, but this chubby Black boy with these glasses and box cut we called 'Bubba,' pushed me in the door before I could make any choice to leave or stay. I covered my face and I wanted to start crying, but Mrs. Jenkin quickly grabbed my hand from my face and gave me a big hug.

All the students in my class were staring at me with smiles and cards. I noticed Bubba went to the back of the classroom and pulled the hand of Andre—this boy I had a crush on—but he never knew.

Andre came right up to me with six red roses and a big class card. I went to put my hand on my face again, but this time Andre pulled my hand and held it. All the students in my class began putting their individual cards on a desk at the front of the class.

"It's ok! I'm sorry to hear 'bout your Mama, but we all missed you!" I couldn't help but smile, even though my heart was heavy. For a long moment, I stood there and felt light.

"Andre, take Kayla to her new seat we made for her! Everyone else, please get settled in your seats." Andre, this skinny caramel skin, Black boy with big, white teeth, led me to my new seat. I had all the cards from everyone on my desk, and a pink balloon tied around the back of my wooden chair. I could barely fit in those damn chairs. There was a bag of snacks filled with Lays chips and Caramilk chocolate—my favourites. I smiled and said thank you, while taking my seat.

Everyone in the class sat looking at me for a good minute, along with Mrs. Jenkin—she quickly picked up a Kleenex from her desk and blew her nose.

"ALRIGHT! Everyone, let's get this morning started. I'm sure it took a lot for Kayla to come here, but we all need to work together to allow her to adjust. I know you are all concerned and want to be there, just please take your time with Kayla. Now let's get started on today's first lesson."

"MAMA, PLEASE!" I screamed in my mind. Mama had one hand covering my mouth and one hand around my neck. She was punishing me for something I had done wrong, and it was a normal routine for her to suffocate me until I couldn't breathe. She did it so whatever I did...I would not even attempt to do it again.

I jumped out my dream, holding my neck with my whole body dripping in cold sweats. I burst into tears when I realized I was only dreaming, curled my body up in a ball in my bed, and tried to put some happy thoughts of Mama in my mind.

My thoughts went blank, and I began crying even more because happy thoughts of Mama and I were not memories we shared—our relationship was cold and distant. It was as if I was a germ of some sort if I did anything to get in Mama's way or to make her upset. Mama wanted everything exactly how she wanted it and if it was not that way, it became a big problem until everything was back to how Mama wanted it.

I got used to just doing exactly what Mama wanted that I never really knew what to do, now that she was gone. I realized Daddy felt the exact same way. Our house was full of silence and we were both just coexisting. It was like Mama had us so conditioned to her way of living, that we lost any path of our own or any voice or mind of our own.

"Kayla baby, you in there?" It was Daddy knocking on my door. I was about to pull the sheets over my head and act like I was sleeping, but before I could, he opened the door.

"Yeah," I said in a mumble.

"I was thinking, maybe we could take a drive into downtown Halifax and go out for dinner. Would you be up for somethin' like that, baby girl? I'm feelin' for a donair from Johnny K's on Blower Street. You up for that?" he said with a big grin, trying to get me to smile.

Daddy was a tall, six foot four, dark skin, brown man. He was muscular with a few tattoos that were fading, and he always dressed in worn down jeans, a plaid shirt of some sort, and construction boots. He had light green eyes, and long curly black hair that he wore back in a ponytail.

The women in North Preston always loved my Daddy, and Mama would always get jealous although Mama was pretty herself. Mama was five foot seven, slim and white, with dark, long, curly brown hair, and blue eyes. She had an hourglass shape and a little bum, which was rare for most white women that I noticed. She had full lips and cat eyes that could sell you anything or cut your heart out if she was mad. Some women in North Preston used to say she was a thicker Angelina Jolie—I don't know who that is, but Mama was pretty, and Daddy always said he loved her from the first time he laid eyes on her.

"So, Pumpkin?" Daddy said, as he walked closer to my bed. He sat down and put his hand on my back, and I turned away from him. I didn't want him to see that I had been crying.

"No, Daddy! I'm ok."

"You sure?"

"Yeah!"

"Alright! I'll bring you back one just in case you wanna eat one later, baby girl. Daddy loves you," he said, and gave me a hug from the back.

He held on for a moment, and I wanted to burst into tears, but I held it. Daddy's love was so genuine and sweet. I just wish he was around a lot more and didn't have to work so much. I loved my Daddy, but I barely ever saw him.

CHAPTER 4: NORTH PRESTON

When you enter the North Preston community one of the first signs you see is 'Canada's Largest Black Community'. I always wondered why they wanted to advertise the race of a community, but then again, I was proud of it. It was (and would always be) my community. There was only one way in...and one way out.

    I asked Daddy that question and he explained that it did. He said North Preston was where the first Black slaves escaped and were free to settle in Canada from the south in the United States of America. He even said some came from Africa and Jamaica.

    After work on the weekends, after Mama died, Daddy would occasionally have some of his cousins come and visit him, and they would always be arguing about the Black people that settled there. Their version was not the same as Granpy's. Uncle Paul (but I called him Mr. Downs) had a completely different version of how Black folks settled in North Preston. He said they were the slaves that escaped from the south in the United States of America and got free in Canada.

Granpy said there was a tribe called the Mi'kmaq Indians that had settled there first, before any slaves arrived from the South. I was confused. Then my Uncle Andre (who I also called Mr. Downs), had a completely wild story that both my Daddy and Uncle Paul would just laugh at. He said that both Granpy and Uncle Paul's stories were true, and that the Mi'kmaq tribe came first to Canada…but they embraced the slaves that settled in Nova Scotia (escaping from the South) and they all got along.

The slaves called North Preston 'Free Town.' He said they all started making babies and teaching each other, when the Scottish invaded to take over. He said names about a war called the 'Gullah Wars' (or some name or another). Uncle Andre said they erased the war from history, because the Indigenous Blacks and Indians defeated the Europeans. He said they defeated the Scottish, but they made a deal with them. The Scottish got to claim the rest of Nova Scotia…but they would give them North Preston and leave them alone on that land—unbothered. That's why we got left in that community by ourselves…and they left us there to govern ourselves.

Uncle Andre said because the slaves and Mi'kmaq tribe could not read or write at that time, they signed ownership of the land away from the Scottish. They were allowed to live on it, but they were never allowed to own the land.

Daddy and my Uncle Paul would just laugh while continuing to drink beer. My Uncle Andre never drank beer, and he always was dressed in the nicest clothes. He had gold chains and gold in his mouth—he was different from the other men Daddy brought over. He was a smooth talker, and always brought me and Mama nice gifts. When Uncle Andre came over, Mama always took him in the room...and was always smiling when they came out.

"You Girl! I see you peepin' out the door! Come on over here, baby girl! Come see your Uncle Dre!" Uncle Andre looked good as usual. He had on all black: leather pants, and a t-shirt with zippers and a leather pocket on the left side at the front. His hair was cut perfectly, with faded lines exactly intact to the shape of his face. His waves were shimmering and perfect with a refreshing scent to match. I could not help but smile.

"I see that smile! Come on over here! I brought you something...You Girl, don't be shy!"

"Hi Uncle Downs," I mumbled, slowly making my way across the living room—it was a complete disaster since Mama left us. Daddy and I were trying to maintain, but with everything going on, Daddy was not keeping up on the chores and I was just not interested in anything at all.

Life had turned into a dream, and the dreams I was having of Mama at night felt like she was haunting me. It was like Mama did not want me to mourn her death—period—but I was lost and numb, and not sure which direction to take. Everything that was normal had disappeared.

The community of North Preston was a very small community. I remember Mrs. Jenkin said one time in class that we had about thirty-five hundred people. Everyone knew everyone, and gossip spread quickly if something happened...but not to the police, though. We knew from a very young age that the police were always the opposite of us in our community, and we were never to trust or talk to them about anything.

I barely trusted anyone, because of Mama. She made it very clear that what you see and hear…you keep to yourself. You don't go around talkin' people's business. She also made it very clear that what happens in our home stays in our home, and it won't be a problem for them to call children's services and get them to come take me away. After years of having that information constantly drilled in my head from when I was five years old, I kept my mouth shut.

In our town, there are two main roads with a lot of small houses and some average sized homes. The houses were older and poorly built—some looked like shacks about to collapse, while others still had a bit of life in them. The people of North Preston had started to rebuild and remodel on the land they lived on themselves, no longer waiting for help from the government (that was never coming).

There are also no businesses in our community, except some locals who owned trucking companies to build our area up. The local fire department—that was the hot spot, where all the guys hung out, along with the church, because we had a big church community. And of course, there were our community organization workers that also supported our Black community.

Daddy would always complain that the government should be giving us ownership of our own land and helping us rebuild our homes. I did not understand this, because I thought we owned our land. But Daddy said we could live on it, but it was not ours… then I remembered what Uncle Downs had said.

We lived around the corner of Simmonds Road and Downey Road. I loved attending the North Preston Community Centre when I was not at school, if Mama would let me—it was just off Simmonds Road, and I could walk. They had all kinds of programs and stuff I could participate in...Mama would just have to get me registered in time. Sometimes she would remember, and sometimes that was not a priority on her list. I loved the cooking classes they offered and also the dance classes.

It was a way to keep my mind occupied and away from my thoughts about Mama. When I was alone, I would always hear her in my mind. Her voice would always find time to end up saying something: "Stop crying!" was what I would hear the most.

I had to get out and be amongst people; Granpy was right. Staying home (and alone) would drive me insane. Mama was all over the place, and even took over my mind, so I would go to the Community Centre to hang out with Bubba and Junior. Uncle Andre would always pick us up after, and drop us home. It wasn't like we couldn't walk, but he was just nice about things.

Uncle Andre had a way with things. He would often check in on Daddy and me after Mama passed. Daddy had to work a lot, driving to the United States, and Granpy couldn't always be around so Uncle Andre would fill in for them to check up on me when I was alone. He would bring his son Andre Jr (but we all called him Junior, or Ice, because he was always eating a cup of Ice or a slushie of some sort).

Ice was the most spoiled kid I met in North Preston. Ever since his Mama left Uncle Andre when he was five years old, Uncle Andre would buy Ice whatever he wanted. He was the only Black kid in North Preston who had a gold chain, earrings in both ears, a blonde dyed box cut fade, and new sneakers every week—whether Jordans or Nikes.

I always wondered what Uncle Andre did as a job, but Daddy said he worked with Pastor Teddy down at the

St. Thomas Baptist Church on Simmonds Road. Anyone who was in North Preston usually went to church. Whether they were feeling good, bad, sad, or mad, they always found time to make service.

Uncle Andre told Ice and I that the slaves escaped to freedom in North Preston generations ago, and that they built the church and passed down the teachings. He told us that we needed to keep spreading the knowledge to each other, and also to future generations. He always said we are a family of brotherhood and sisterhood. I saw the brotherhood of Daddy and all my uncles…but the sisterhood I was not quite aware of.

I mean, they came to church—they cooked, baked, sang, gossiped, and took care of their men (while going to bingo or fighting) but that was all that I witnessed. Us young girls were no part of any sisterhood.

The young boys in our community were different: they stayed after the church service was done with the grown men. Not all of the boys, but a select few. Ice was one of them, but he did not seem interested—he looked pressured to stay because Uncle Andre was there. I always wondered what they talked about. Mama would always rush me out the big white wooden church doors saying, "A young lady ain't got no place being in a grown man's business, let alone grown folk's business!"

There was one day I remember, I went to church after Mama had died, and I forgot my bag inside the church after service finished. I was halfway home down Simmonds Road when I realized and turned back. When I arrived at the church (that looked like a fancy house that someone painted to live in, more than it did a church), I approached the doors. Before I could open them, Bubba came running out. His pants were halfway down, and he was pulling up his underwear, crying. I went to ask him what was wrong, but he kept on crying and running down Simmonds Road before I got the chance.

The church doors flung open, and Uncle Andre's eyes and mine met. I froze in my tracks, and he gave me the scariest look I had ever seen from a man in my life! The look was evil, as if he was a different person. His eyes were dark, and I was so scared that I ran down Simmonds Road and didn't even bother about getting my bag from the church.

We were all in junior high now, attending Graham Creighton Junior High School.

I never ever told anyone about that day—not Granpy or Daddy. I just kept that story to myself.

Bubba never returned to church again, and his family moved away from North Preston a short time after. Bubba was such a happy kid; he was the class clown and everyone in the school loved Bubba. Bubba and Ice were best friends, but whatever happened at the church that day changed them both. It ruined their friendship and they both started acting differently. Bubba stopped talking, and Ice just became real mean. He would steal a lot for no reason (he had money, so there was no motive for him to steal). Ice started beating on girls and pulling their hair. Kids started gossiping that he was burning cats and raping girls. Every girl he got alone, he forced them to have sex with him, or he would beat them up.

The girls in North Preston stopped speaking to me, because Ice treated me differently—he would leave me alone or was quiet around me. He would even give me things or buy me candy or food. It was kinda cute, but I figured it was just because he was family to me and he felt like he could relate because both our Mamas were gone. The girls saw it completely differently, however, and isolated me altogether. They would gossip about me, make fun of me, and gossip about my Mama being a drug addict saying how she overdosed on drugs, and that's why she died. It was just cruel and evil. They made me feel like a complete outcast. I hated school at that point.

One day I was in the washroom having lunch when I heard two girls from my classroom talking. I raised my feet up off the bathroom floor and stood on the toilet, so they could not see that anyone was in the washroom. Sasha and Laquita were gossiping about how Sasha heard her dad telling her uncle how my Uncle Andre was dealing my Mama heroin. She said how my Uncle Andre was fucking my Mama, too, and had been for a long time...and that my Daddy probably didn't even know.

They left the bathroom laughing, and I sat in the bathroom sobbing for the rest of that lunch period, vomiting out what I just ate. I cried and could not take it any longer, so I ran out of the school, all the way home to my house. I could not believe what I had just heard! I was so confused. Did Daddy even know any of this? Mama was on drugs? Mama was fuckin' Uncle Andre? Did Granpy know? I remember Uncle Andre always saying 'cousins makes dozens,' but I thought it was just an old Nova Scotian joke.

Where was Daddy when I needed him? The tears started rolling down my face uncontrollably, and I wanted to scream for Mama.

I laid there on the brown couch Mama died on, and started crying even harder, when the door knocked. I ignored it, but the knocking continued and only got louder.

"IT'S ME, ICE! ANSWER THE DOOR!" Even though I did not want Ice to be family, I opened the door.

"What do you want, Junior? I need to be left alone," I said as I opened the front door. Ice barged in and immediately walked past me to my room. He was holding something in his hand, covered in a red blanket, but I did not have a chance to see what it was.

"COME! Let me show you what I just got," he said as he sat down on my bed with a big smile on his face.

"What, Junior! What is it?"

"This!" He pulled off the red blanket and a black gun sat there on his lap.

"Where did you...?" I started to get freaked out, but Ice put his hand over my mouth.

"Just listen! Daddy gave me this. Said he's hearing bad things about you and me. Said I need to keep this if anyone tries anything. He said I have to protect our family at all costs."

"Uncle Andre gave you that?"

"Yes. I also heard about you running off school property, crying. Some of the stuff people are talking about is true. I asked Daddy. He said he loved your Mama and will always love her. He said he took care of her the nights your Daddy couldn't."

"STOP! STOP! STOP!"

"You have to know! Or else they are gonna keep talking, and making you feel worse. He told me we may even be brother and sister. I knew; I always knew this. That's why I protected you and never treated you like other girls. You are special, and I love you more than you will ever know." He put his head down. It was so weird; I wanted to hold him. I had feelings for Ice, but this changed everything.

"Do you know for a fact this is true?"

"I said it could be. I don't know for sure."

"Is Uncle Andre gonna tell Daddy?"

"He said one day, but not any time soon because it would hurt him badly."

"He told me to give you this as well, and for you to come by the church this weekend!"

He handed me a bundle of cash, and a gold diamond Cuban link bracelet engraved with my initials. I was at a loss for words, but I had to find out the truth. I had to find out the truth from Uncle Andre.

"You ok?" he asked, with the softest of sincerity in his voice. His eyes were a small almond shape, and he must have got the green eye colour from his mama. Ice was so good looking and had such a sweetheart. I could not help but fall under a spell.

"Ya, I'm ok," I said in a quiet mumble, and began to look away from his gaze of love…but Ice (with the gun in his right hand) pulled me closer to him with his left. I just froze, not in fear of the gun, but in fear of what was next.

Ice leaned in and gave me the first kiss I ever received from a boy. I could really hear Mama now…but I could not move. My legs were frozen, but at the time I felt like I was about to drop. Ice turned around and put the gun down on the red cloth that he placed on my bed.

He turned his attention to me and started kissing me with so much love. I started to return the kisses. It felt so good. He began kissing my neck and slid his hand up my shirt.

"Stop, Ice!"

"What do you mean stop? You know you want this just as much as me!"

"Ya, but we could be family! Like, blood related."

"Just forget I told you that! I love you a lot, and I want you to be my girl." His words stuck to my heart, but something was wrong. I pushed him back off of me and he fell on the bed—by accident, he landed on the gun and it went off when he tried to grab it.

We both jumped, frightened, but luckily it was just a hole in the wall from the bullet. Our eyes locked in a wild passionate bliss from what we had just witnessed, but the innocence of our inexperience was too young to understand our feelings.

"Come, I want to show you somethin'." Ice pulled my hand, nudging me towards the front of my house. He cleared up his belongings off my bed and led me towards the doorway.

"Where are we going?"

"Do you trust me?" He looked into my eyes with so much love and warmth that my whole body started to tingle.

"Yes...I..."

"Come on then!"

What Ice showed me later that day will go to my grave with me.

CHAPTER 5: HIGH SCHOOL

High school was another place that I did not belong. I was an outcast, especially being bi-racial. The white kids thought I would give them information on people from North Preston, and once they realized I wouldn't, they excluded me quickly from their circles. The kids from North Preston thought I was getting favoured over them because the teachers tried to get me to rat on my own…but it never happened.

Ice was my only savior, again. He had all the kids at school admiring him because he was the school dope dealer. He got invited to all the white kids' parties and hustled them out of all their money. The Black kids from North Preston loved him because Uncle Andre was the OG of North Preston, and Ice was his up-and-coming son behind him. He had everyone's respect on the block. He still protected me, but at the same time he made it known that I had a place as a 'girl' in an indirect way. He made time for me when it suited him—and at his convenience—but yet he never let anyone violate or disrespect me ever, or they would pay for it in the worst way.

People still talked about me behind my back constantly, but when Ice was around they kissed the ground I walked on and acted like they were my friends. The fake bullshit disgusted me. All I ever really wanted was to sing and be accepted for who I was, but ever since Mama passed away it was like I never got to figure out who I was. Everything stopped for me. Mama never had anything good to say about me, Daddy was always at work, and Granpy's health was getting worse as time passed so…where did that leave me?

It left me confused about who I was as a teenager with absolutely no guidance. I continued to follow Ice around like a puppy dog that was loyal and longing for his acceptance, from him, and whoever would give it. I tried to focus on school, but the more I was outcast by the rest of my classmates, the more I internalized those feelings and began to act out in other ways.

I started dressing more provocatively and started to do things that I thought would get me accepted.

My teachers noticed the difference in my behaviour and tried to contact Daddy, but he was on the road so much that he never returned their calls. I had a freedom that a young teenager at my age with no guidance (and in such a vulnerable state) should not have.

"There's a party this weekend—you coming? Everyone's goin' be there!" Ice asked, counting all his money he made from a day of hustling at school.

"I got homework to do, and I don't like or talk to half of those people…so why would I go?" I said not to give him any attention, and I continued to write in my songwriting book. I was working on this new song for Mama that I wanted to perform at the church. I wanted to get back into my singing because I had been missing it.

Ice slapped the book out my hand.

"WHAT THE FUCK IS YOUR PROBLEM? You and that damn book! Always in that damn book!" he said, laughing, but I knew he was trying to hide his anger.

"You're so fuckin annoying sometimes. Like for real. Leave my stuff alone!"

"What do you mean by your stuff? If I didn't give you the money, you couldn't even buy it! All the things I buy for you and take you places…I don't ask you for shit, but to at least act like you like me when we are around other people. I protect you and make sure no one does anything to you. I'm trying to make them respect you, but you're not making it easy," he said, softening his voice. Ice had a way of charming me into doing things because he always had my back.

"What do you mean act?" I said, sounding as naive as possible.

"Like this." He pushed himself forward, leaned in, and kissed me on the lips. I froze. I didn't know if I should slap him or lean in for more.

He smiled and kissed me again, but this time he slipped his tongue in my mouth and put his hand on my breast.

"Ice! Please, just..." I couldn't get the words out, and before I knew it, Ice was on top of me, pulling all my clothes off. It felt so good that I didn't know how to stop him—then I felt this pressure inside of me, and heard him breathing heavily.

"I knew all this time...you wanted this inside you." And it was done.

"Now you my girl, and I own you!"

"WHAT?" I pushed him off me and realized his penis pulled out of my vagina. I was bleeding a little bit, but that was not what I wanted to happen. I was so caught up in the moment, I didn't even realize Ice pushed his penis inside of me and broke my virginity.

"We are together now! You are my girl. I just broke your virginity, and now no one can have you but me!" He smiled.

"Ice, I never wanted to do..."

"WHAT? What you tryin' to say? Yo, you wanted it, and don't talk that shit to me!" His eyes switched and he looked angry. He came close to my face, and it was like a different person was in the room. I was scared. I backed up on the bed, naked and vulnerable. I could not move. He grabbed the gun off the floor with his money.

"That's a good girl! You see all of this?" I nodded my head, shivering. "It's all yours now. You're my girl and you have to act like it, and what I say...you do. Now spread those legs open, and let me get some more." I shook my head not to disagree, but his look of anger got worse. His face was even more of a rage. He took the gun, put a bullet in the chamber, and aimed it at my head. "Open those legs for your Daddy?" Daddy? I was so in fear of what was happening, and just did what I was told. His penis was so hard—he slid it inside me and kept the gun at my head. "That's my good girl," he said over and over, until he pulled out while releasing himself all over my stomach.

I never told anyone; I knew never to cross him. I also knew I had to play my part so he wouldn't treat me that way again. He loved me, and he just wanted me to show it. I was his baby, and I was only hurting him by not showing him the love he was showing me.

●

"You look good in that dress, baby! You like it?" Ice asked, as we walked up to the door of some white kid's party. You could hear the music blaring from down the street, and there were all kinds of Ford trucks and bikes parked outside.

The house looked like a cabin in the middle of the woods in some part of Dartmouth, Nova Scotia. Uncle Andre gave Ice his old black Cadillac 2005 truck for his sixteenth birthday, so Ice felt like he was the king of North Preston. Everyone at school continued to kiss his ass like he was the king, and he sure started to act even more like an asshole...but not towards me. I just did what he said, and he was cool.

He gave me everything I wanted. As long as we had sex all the time and I sucked his dick (whenever he wanted, however he wanted), he did everything for me. He was so sweet to me and made sure everyone else was always taken care of. Uncle Andre was giving me gifts and buying me nice clothing, and I was never home.

He made sure he communicated with Daddy about taking care of me, and he checked on Granpy. He had the women from the church (who were staying with Granpy) make sure Granpy was good. I tried to go up there, but he said Granpy was not taking visitors at the time. I was sad about it, but I understood his health and aging. I stayed at the house, and Uncle Andre had me counting money a lot with Ice…but I wasn't sure where all the money came from. I just stayed minding my business, and did as I was told. I didn't want Ice to ever get angry again.

"Yes, I like the dress. Thank you, baby!" I said, snapping out of my thoughts. Ice grabbed onto my shoulders and started giving me a massage when some drunk white kid named Derrick (from my math class) opened the door.

"WELL, IF IT ISN'T KAYLA AND THE ICEMAN! Come on in. Hey…ICE IS HERE!" he said, almost tripping over his own feet. He was a short white dude that had a shaved bald head…and no shirt on. He was wearing dark, ripped jeans with white paint splashed all over them, and had on some broken down working man's boots that you wear to do construction. His hair was in a long messy blond ponytail that had not been combed in Lord knew how long.

Ice and I entered the house—that smelled of sweaty armpits, Doritos, beer, and cheesy feet mixed with cigarettes—and I almost vomited at the nasty smell. Ice saw the look on my face.

"It's for money, baby! You Girl, don't think 'bout nothin' else...you here for me. I got something real nice for you after. Here, take this." Ice handed me a baby blue pill that had an 'S' on it.

"What's this, baby?"

"Jus' somethin' to relax you and make the time go by! I take them when you don't come with me."

"Ok." I figured if Ice took it...it was all good. I popped the pill in my mouth just in time. There was Derrick, stumbling across the packed living room, bumping into people before he handed us two halves of two beers.

"Why the fuck the beers half empty? Go back and get two more full closed beers!" Ice said, taking the two beers from Derrick's hand and throwing them to the ground, causing them to smash into pieces. The music shut off immediately and everyone turned their attention to Ice.

"Baby, it's ok. It's just two..."

"SIT THE FUCK DOWN AND SHUT UP! DIS GROWN MEN SHIT!" He pushed me on the couch, and I knew this was the Ice I did not like. I put my head down because I did not want him to continue disrespecting me.

"Hey man, it's just beer, and don't disrespect fuckin' women like that. Didn't your mom ever teach you how to treat women?" I covered my face completely, and sunk down into the black leather couch (that you know every girl they brought here got fucked on), to feel a beer bottle under my ass. I wanted to pull it out, but who knew what else was underneath.

"What the fuck you boy say 'bout my mama?" Ice walked closer without saying a word, and everyone froze in silence.

"Nothin'! It was a joke. Lighten up."

"Yo! Don't let me fuckin' smash this bottle over your head, you boy!" Ice walked closer to Derrick and backhanded him with the loudest slap across the face...even I felt like I got slapped, by how loud it was.

"WHAT THE FUCK?" Derrick screamed.

"For anyone else in here, this is a fuckin' warning. You muthafuckas understand me? Drunk or fuckin' not, don't disrespect me or my girl—period! Y'all get out of line again, and this is what you're gonna get!" Ice pulled out his gun from his waist, and pointed at Derrick. "Get on your fuckin' knees now, you boy!"

No one moved; everyone sat watching Ice in complete horror. Derrick dropped to his knees, crying and sobbing at this point. Ice put the gun to his head.

"Do you muthafuckas understand?" He looked around at everyone, and then started pointing the gun around the room. Everyone in the room shook their heads 'yes,' in fear of being shot or hurt by Ice. "Now y'all understand! I run this fuckin' town, and if you want anything or need anything, you come to me!" He put his gun back in his pants and started to smile. "Get up, you boy! Look what you made me do, man! I was just playing with you, but don't ever disrespect me by bringing up my Mamma. You understand?"

"Yes man. I'm sorry! Derrick said, cowering down to Ice.

"It's all good—you my boy. Let's not make that happen again. Cool?" Ice reached out his hand, and Derrick hesitated. He eventually shook his hand in fear. Everyone knew Ice had become a loose cannon and would pop off anytime someone crossed him.

"DJ, let's get back down to business! Run the music, you boy!" The DJ did what he was told (in fear), but the good vibes of the party were ruined. Everyone tried to act like they were ok, but we all knew the only person in the party that was ok was Ice.

I started to feel like I was on a cloud, and everything started to feel dreamy—the music was playing like I never heard music before. I got up and started dancing. The music was taking over my body and I could not stop dancing. I must have made some impression, because people started dancing around with me. Ice started dancing a little bit too, and then he disappeared while I continued dancing. My spirit came alive as the music and my soul became one. I was in complete euphoria—anything and everything had disappeared in that moment. I was in love with the feeling, and wanted more.

CHAPTER 6: WHITNEY HOUSTON

There are pieces of your heart that get taken away with each moment of pain that inflicts it deeply. I wanted to love and be free...but my world was changing by the moment, and my heart was sinking deeper into isolation the more life consumed me. I was turning into someone I did not know. I was never home, and was always on the road with Ice, from Dartmouth to North Preston. He worked and I followed, while beginning to study hustling.

From Uncle Andre to Ice, I was learning the game of drugs, pimpin', and how the church was our home as much as our savior to escape things. I knew Uncle Andre had more going on with the church...but that was none of my business. In North Preston, we were a family that looked out for each other because the government left us to starve by ourselves in an isolated community. We did what we had to do to make it—by any means necessary. Hangin' out at the fire station gettin' lit and protecting' our community; everyone was in competition for the top spot.

By this time I was barely in school, and Ice already dropped out to make money. The only education he had interest in was from the School of Hard Knocks, and with his daddy as his mentor, he learned everything he could possibly learn.

There was one big difference between Ice and Uncle Andre's personalities: Uncle Andre had a way with people in the community—actually anyone—he spoke to. He made everyone feel important, and it always had people eating right out of his hands and doing anything he needed.

Ice, on the other hand, was an uncontrollable thug that wanted to learn and control the game so badly...but always had setbacks because of his anger issues. Ice bullied his way for control, while Uncle Andre charmed people into giving their power and control to him with mind manipulation.

They were a power team together, but apart...Uncle Andre was always having to clean up Ice's immature mistakes. He would punish Ice for a while, getting him to stay home and hold the fort down, but eventually he realized Ice brought in a lot of money in the streets. In a twisted way, it was like Uncle Andre was training Ice to become the thug that he was...but indirectly acting like it was all Ice's fault.

I sat on the sidelines, and just did as I was told, not wanting to get in the center of that mess (even though they tried pulling me in the middle when they had fights). Uncle Andre would tease Ice about how he could take me away from him in a minute. He would joke about it all the time, but eventually it did not seem like a joke anymore. We all laughed, but Uncle Andre meant it, and it infuriated Ice. Eventually, Uncle Andre had me with him all the time while Ice was doing errands.

There was a power I started to feel being around Uncle Andre because I was protected, made a lot of money, and Ice would not disrespect me in front of him. I also started to gain a lot of respect from North Preston, but there were also conversations circulating that I was fucking Uncle Andre, which was the farthest thing from the truth.

The more the rumors spread, the more Ice became angry towards Uncle Andre and I. He hated not having control and power over Uncle Andre. He hated that he had to take instructions like some errand boy, while Uncle Andre told everyone what needed to be done. He was jealous of Uncle Andre's power, love, and respect that came naturally.

Ice started a crew of his own friends that were our age group and wanted to make money, just like Uncle Andre showed Ice how to do. They called themselves North Preston Savages. Ice, being the leader of his 'family,' started operations (pimpin' and drug dealing) all over Nova Scotia, leaving North Preston for Uncle Andre to lead. The more Ice was focused on hustling and his crew, the more he ignored me. I started to hear stories of different girls he was using to work with him; we would fight, and he would say they were just there to make him money. But I knew there was more to it.

Uncle Andre would always console me when I was upset, and we became closer the more distant Ice became. I was in love with Ice, but the harder I fell for him...the more distant he became.

"You Girl! Pass me that counter. I need us to clear up all this inventory and have it recorded in the system before Ice gets back. You lose a lot of focus when that boy of mine is around; I see the fear that he has instilled in you. You do realize you make more money together in love than in fear?" Uncle Andre grabbed my cheek and kissed it. He then put a twenty-four karat, diamond, Cuban link bracelet in front of me. I looked surprised...yet felt uncomfortable.

"This is for your hard work. You have done a lot of good work here. Have you ever thought about making more money?"

"Thank you, Uncle Andre. You didn't have to," I paused in disbelief. The bracelet was beautiful and full of diamonds. I honestly felt like a queen. "I don't feel comfortable accepting this! Ice is gonna get pissed off and wanna fight about it."

"This is a gift from him and I. He already knows. I spoke to him about it before he left, so there is no need to worry about Ice."

"Are you sure? I love it! As for more money...what do you suggest? What else is there for me to do?" Uncle Andre smiled, and then made a weird noise sounding like some villain cartoon character who just captured the hero. It was deep, dark, and not funny at all. He must have sensed my uncomfortable vibe because he quickly stopped laughing.

"I am sure, because everyone that is a part of my team has one...including Ice. As for work, I need someone to watch over Ice while I'm out of town next week. I'm going to Vancouver for a few weeks. I would bring you, but we know Ice is a loose cannon. Who knows what mess I would come back to when I got back."

"What makes you think anyone can watch over Ice? That boy has a mind of his own, and when he's angry, all of his ration goes out the window."

"Well, that's where you come in. I'm going to leave him with some work for me, but I am letting him know that he has to include you in all my operations. If I could trust my own son, I would not need you...but I can't. And with Miss Betty in Alberta holding it down for me out there, I can't risk Ice fucking up anymore business."

"I understand." I assembled my new bracelet on my wrist with a smile. A part of me felt like I had just found a home away from Daddy, Granpy, and Mama. It was like a whole new chapter of my life was beginning.

"That looks perfect on you, don't you think? Now you are locked to our family for life. They say cousins make dozens, but I say if you build it...they will come. Just like what Pastor says at church."

I got lost in the possibilities and future paths I could take to find my way to happiness. Sometimes I would catch myself thinking of Granpy and then start singing or humming songs that we would sing together. How I missed him!

"Any news on how Granpy is doing, and when I can go see him?"

Uncle Andre paused before answering, and that's when I knew he was about to come with an animated version of some story. Any time Uncle Andre paused in thought before answering my question (or anyone else's for that matter), he was thinking of some way to over exaggerate the story.

"Right, Christ chile! I forgot to tell you! When I get back, you are going to see and spend some time with your Granpy. He's been asking about you a lot lately: his 'Lily,' as he calls you. I'll bring you to see him when I get back!"

Things drastically changed when Uncle Andre left town. I was trying to manage the money coming in like he asked, but Ice was upset and jealous that he even put me in that type of role. Part of me wonders 'til this day if it was a plan of Uncle Andre's, but I will never know. Ice was an angry thug that went around tormenting people, while Uncle Andre manipulated situations for his own benefit.

I thought it could have been a setup because Ice switched, and was treating me like a prisoner. He would not let me eat certain things or speak to anyone but him, yet he always made sure I was doped up on those pills. One night he had a bag of coke laying around on the table where the money counter was, and I was so high that I got curious and decided to try it. I knew it was cocaine but I had wondered what the high felt like.

I took the hundred-dollar bill, rolled it up, and decided to try some. I didn't know how much to pour out, so of course being high and curious...I poured out too much.

"Shit!" Ice was in the driveway; I could hear his rap music playing from his Cadillac, so I quickly snorted it all up before he could realize that I sampled it. Worst mistake ever. Before I knew it, my heart was racing and I felt like I could dance and run a mile all in the same step. My heartbeat kept, fluttering all over the place. Ice (being a dealer and all) must have known, because he went right to the bag and then looked at me.

"You touch this bag? You Girl!" I tried to hide that I was bouncing off the walls, but he knew. "You Girl, you don't hear me talking to you? Didn't I teach you anything? You never get high off your own supply unless I give it to you!"

"I just wanted to know what it was."

He paused—looking at me in disgust—then grabbed the bag of cocaine and started pouring it on the table.

"Come here, baby girl. You want to try it? I'll show you just how to do it." He poured a long line across the table and told me to snort it all up my nose.

"Isn't that too much?"

"Do it! NOW!" I jumped up and did as I was told. I made my way to the table in hesitation but knew he would hit me if I did not. I snorted it all and could taste it down my throat. My ears started ringing and my nose started bleeding. I started seeing everything blurry and dropped to the floor, passing out. "Stupid idiot! Wait 'til Pops hear about this bullshit. You won't be his angel now, will you?"

I woke up on the floor in the same position, except I had no underwear on and there was a condom on the floor. My head was pounding and I needed to pull myself together before Ice or anyone came around. When I got in the washroom and got undressed, I saw bruises all over my body. I wanted to cry but realized it was all due to my own stupidity. I could hear Mama now: "You just a slut like them easy girls from around the way! You ain't no chil' of mine, acting like that!"

CHAPTER 7: SNATCHED

Fall in Nova Scotia is one of the most beautiful things to watch. I remember the days I would roll in the orange- and yellow-coloured leaves, trying to hide. The change of the seasons in nature was so beautiful. I would bury myself so deep in a pile of leaves that when the sun was shining, I could see the rays of sunshine highlighting the leaves and all the rhythmic patterns. I remember Granpy telling me the world was full of patterns, and if I remained present in the moment, I could find my purpose in the patterns.

"Everything has a pattern—it's all connected from God to the Universe...all the way down to us. We are all connected to this pattern. It's the pattern of divine greatness."

I must have been dreaming; it was a reality when my phone rang. I grabbed it off the night table beside the bed.

"Hello?" I said, wiping the sleep out of my eyes, trying to see clearly. I looked over to see Ice lying beside me in a deep sleep—I didn't even remember him coming in last night.

"My dearest Lily! How are you? I have missed you so much!" My eyes immediately started filling up with water and tears began rolling down my face.

"Granpy?"

"Yes, it's Granpy! I know I have not been doing well, but I'm starting to feel better. I want you to come up and see me. Sooner than later. We need to talk in person about a few things. When can you come visit?"

"Um, I'm not sure. I'll try to come for the weekend. I was going to wait until Uncle Andre came back to town to come and see you."

"No! I need you to come in the next couple days. I have something to speak to you about and I have something to give you. It is important. I had a dream about you—this is necessary. Please come sooner than later."

"Ok. I'll try to come over the weekend. Is everything ok?"

"We will talk when I see you. Take care for now."

"Ok bye, Granpy. I love you."

"Bye, Lily. I love you too." I sat on the phone waiting for Granpy to hang up and I wanted to burst into tears. I looked over and Ice was watching me, so I swallowed all the tears down my throat.

"Why are you cryin? It's not like you barely see the man. You're crying like you're dyin' or some shit...or like he is! You really gotta learn to wake up. People come and go just like we will, so there's no need to cry over this shit! Just accept it and live your life making millions so no one can tell you what to do you. You have the freedom to do what the fuck you want. You know I love you right? And will always be here to take care of you?" Ice started kissing on my cheek and I wanted to melt in his arms. I just wished he was like that all the time. "I got some great news! We are gonna take a trip down to Toronto soon to expand the business."

I paused, looking deep into Ice's hazel, brown, almond shaped eyes. I wanted to see if those child eyes filled with joy when they saw me, but Ice's eyes were cold and distant. He barely looked into my eyes and when he had 'great news,' it was never great news, and we always ended up in some situation that Uncle Andre had to bail Ice out of. And then Ice would end up blaming me for it.

My mind was worried about Granpy. That's the only reason why I wasn't consumed with entertaining Ice and his ideas or get rich quick schemes. He was Uncle

Andre's top soldier but he always wanted to be the boss. He hated listening to Uncle Andre. I was more concerned about what Granpy had to tell me.

"Cat got your tongue, You Girl? I need some mornin' lips on my dick right now. Come give Daddy some love."

I did as I was told. Usually if I could keep Ice in a good mood from the morning, it lasted all day and I didn't have to argue or do things that would have him acting like an asshole all day.

"Ok, baby! When are we leaving?"

"Tonight."

"Ice, I have to go and see Granpy before we leave. It's important, and he has something he wants to tell me. I feel like something's wrong. I need to go before we leave." I was unbuckling Ice's pants to give him oral sex when I felt him pull my hair and yank me off the bed, onto the floor.

"Right Christ, You Girl! You don't fuckin' listen when I tell you. You do what I fuckin' say! Now shut up and do what I fuckin' asked of you before you get me upset." The rage in his eyes! I was afraid, but something inside of me spoke up for Granpy.

"Ice, I'm going to see my Granpy—something is not ok with him right now!" I did not look at him when I spoke. I kept my eyes on the ground. All of a sudden, I felt my head get yanked right into Ice's face.

"Did you hear what I said? I said you ain't goin' no fuckin' place. Now be a good girl and give Daddy what he needs, 'cause you're not the only girl that wants me, you know! I can get my dick sucked anywhere…but I chose you. So do what I'm askin' and stop makin' shit hard. You want to be my wife and you want to have my kids and we make millions, right? Well you gotta take care of me and you gotta put in work too, like I have been."

"What do you mean work?"

"I got a job for you when we get down to Toronto. You are gonna be my head bitch in charge and set up shop and run the business with me. Don't you want that for us, baby?"

"Yes Daddy, that's what I want! Oh my gosh, why did you hide this from me?"

"Shhhhh! Just be a good girl to Daddy right now! I want to show you just how much I love you."

Ice's childlike eyes surfaced back, looking deep into my eyes, and my heart felt heavy. I wanted to cry. He really did love me and had plans for us and our future. He really meant what he said: he was just trying to protect me and build a life with me. He flipped me over on the bed and ripped my panties off.

"You are mine. I own you!"

"Yes, my Daddy!"

CHAPTER 8: ICE

My Daddy always said don't love no hoe, but Kayla was not a hoe. She was from a North Preston family. I mean cops, the media, and the news always try to portray any Black muthafucka out here tryna get money as a threat or a gang, when these muthafuckas push us in the slums without shit and expect us not to figure out a way to get shit. My grandfather was a pimp, and my Daddy a pimp, and my cousins are pimps...so what the fuck you think I'm gonna be? A fuckin' pimp. I learned the game from the best and it's what I know. Break ah hoe and get some more.

Kayla was different. I loved that girl from the first time I saw her, at the age of five. I wanted to marry her. She was different from the other girls around the way. She was smart...but sometimes too smart for her own good, and she never knew how to listen or take instructions.

I'm a man. Daddy always told me a woman has to know her place in this game and she's to do what I say. Daddy was too nice about it. I ain't got time for all that. I ask once and you don't listen...then that's your choice, but like I said with Kayla...it was different. I would hurt her, feel bad about it, and then get her everything she wants. Then I would tell her my feelings and show her more of the game and she would fuck up again and I would get upset again. If she would just listen and not be so fuckin' stubborn, we would already be millionaires. All she had to do was just play her damn part. I already had the rest.

Kayla was convinced she was going to be a singer but she had to understand where we came from. No one cared about us in North Preston but us. We were a family and we loved our own. We protected our own, but when the money started coming in...then the jealousy and envy started coming in. Niggas started gettin' flashy and the police came runnin' in our community when before we policed ourselves. They just made shit worse and started comparing us to other organized gangs all over Canada just because we stated where we came from—but that was all some bullshit.

They never realized it was the same fuckin' white man my ancestors ran from in them dirty muddy waters in them dark nights to freedom following the moon as their only light to see. Harriet Tubman with the underground railroad, helping to free my people with no shoes—some no clothes—or who knows if we would have been alive today. We had absolutely fuckin' nothing on our back yet they wanted to label us as drug dealing killers, and some big ass organized gang, yet these muthafuckas have the world's wealth and leave the rest of us Black Indigenous People of Colour to starve and find our way.

Then when we do find a way...we are the problem. My question is, were they trying to give us a voice or a hand...or anything to this date? How the fuck did the drugs get here? Cuz it sure ain't us who have access to the planes to fly 'em here, and it sure ain't us who is paying billions of dollars for the pussy that's being sold, and this is a billion dollar industry! For the guns that are here (and been here) and please let me remind you once again we are in poverty so WHO gave us access to all this shit and what was the purpose?

We have always been their prey...but why kill ourselves off or kill each other? They did it in Oakland with the CIA and the Mexicans, but to us, they wanna label us as a threat. They introduced the crack cocaine pandemic. Wake the fuck up. You can either be the prey or the predator, that's what my Granpy always said.

Who is THEY you ask? They hide and lurk in the shadows. They prey and feed off the masses. They are the privileged muthafuckas that fed our ancestors the poisons while they raped their women and stole our jewels. They are the ones that have no origin and if they do, please tell me where it comes from? Why do they have a calcified pineal gland but the Black Womb-AN has the 'EVE' gene?

My Granpy taught me all this shit, and yet people think I'm just some angry young Black nigga with no sense. Hell no! I see shit very clearly. I'm taking it all back for what they did to me and my ancestors...but not just that. I realized also...you create your own reality, because how the fuck did them muthafuckas create that shit for so many years and we believed it? Some of us are still programmed under this dark cloud of oppression—we can barely survive to make it to another day. We are lost within ourselves so much that we have no clue where we have come from...so how would we realize where we are going, or even where we are at right now?

I thought about this shit all the time, and the rage inside of me grew higher at each moment. The more I saw the bigger picture, I realized I could eat...or I could get eaten. But for the Black man, there was never a choice after slavery began. They have been preying on us since then, and continue to do so. We have been fighting that death sentence since we came out of our mother's wombs.

Born into a prison, bondage, and caged. Humiliated for the colour of your skin and your features that do not reflect other races. I was proud to come from North Preston and be Black, but I also believe that proud God-fearing confidence can get you killed! You can be breathing the wrong way and end up in a ditch—chopped and buried because you are a threat to a superior wealthy race, who demonizes the origin of your roots while stripping away any recollection of who you are. Leaving you in a vulnerable state of illusion where it is easy to victimize a person who can't see. What you choose once you realize your path is your choice.

I chose it. I chose me. I chose North Preston.

"You Girl! Kayla! I don't know what is wrong with this chick? I tell her something and she always has to have her own mind. Doing the most to disobey me when I take care of her the most!"

The house was hollow, damp, and empty. The paintings Daddy had were of him and his hoes, all over the walls mixed with leather furniture pieces and Persian rugs. He always had to show off. That's one characteristic where we differ—I ain't about all the floss type shit but where the fuck was Kayla?

"You know who dis is! Leave a message."

"I swear for fuck sakes, man! Now I gotta go try to find this bitch. Get on my damn fuckin' nerves." I started texting when the phone rang.

"I LISTEN TO YOUR STUPID FUCKIN' ASS AND MY GRANPY IS DEAD! I DIDN'T GET TO SAY GOODBYE!"

"Calm down, Kayla! You Girl, calm fuck down!"

"YOU CALM THE FUCK DOWN AND FUCK OFF!"

Before I spoke, Kayla hung up. One thing she lost was her Granpy—and I have compassion for that—but if I let her think she can talk to me this way, she will continue. I gotta take her away for a few days before we leave town. I need to put this girl in check and get her mind right for business. She has this victim mentality, and scared money don't make no money.

North Preston was a very solid community. We are all family, so it took me no time to find Kayla at Uncle

Frank's. Uncle Frank was an old-time musician that played blues and jazz, amongst other things. I remembered when DMX came to town, he was chillin' with Uncle Frank. Daddy told me they talked about music for hours. I knew Kayla would be there, 'cause she could sing, drink, and get high. Uncle Frank partied, so we all knew the flex if you were hanging at his house. He also never let any drama happen in his house. Kayla knew I would have to get her out of there before I said or did anything. Best option was to feed them both dope, and take Kayla out of there. Get her safe so she can rest and have a moment to grieve her Granpy.

    I pulled up to Uncle Frank's house. You could tell he was one of the oldest in North Preston because he has so many memories of things we couldn't witness. He kept us educated on the musical background that came out of Nova Scotia and North Preston, but he also educated us on how music was therapy—an escape and a gift that we possessed to free us from the mental, emotional, or physical prisons we were enslaved in. Uncle Frank would always say, 'let the music set you free.'

    I could hear Kayla signing, just like the days she would be in the church choir. Her voice was powerful, and she did have talent, but ain't no one trying to help us down here. We have to help ourselves. All that signing and no money is some broken man's dream type shit. I ain't got time for all that nonsense.

    I walked in the front door and before I could even speak, Uncle Frank looked at me as if he would kill me. This short, dark-skinned Black man (with all his front teeth missing, and clothes looking like he hadn't changed them for a few days) wore a stained white t-shirt with food and drinks from the past previous days of meals. He had a battered down Maple Leafs hat on that was barely sitting on his head.

I didn't say a word; I just let Kayla sing her lungs 4out. It was like some kind of magic was happening between the two of them when Uncle Frank stopped the music.

"That was the one! You starlight! That was the take I was looking for! We got a hit on our hands, Ice."

"What you mean, Uncle Frank?"

"Ice, why do you always gotta ruin shit?"

"Get in the car Kayla, and don't let me ask twice. Uncle Frank, pass the recording now."

"You Boy! I told you no drama here!" Uncle Frank stormed towards me, but before he could get one word out of his twitching mouth, I pulled out a bag of cocaine. Uncle Frank stopped.

"You can't buy me, Ice Cream! Now go get you a Sunday, and get the fuck on. As for this recording...it stays here. You have a problem, call your Daddy, or Kayla's. Oh that's right...you can't call Kayla's Daddy, 'cause he don't know the bullshit you've been doing to her! Get on, You Boy, before I pull out my shotgun and shit gets real."

"You gonna do me like that, Uncle Frank?"

"Haven't we taught you anything, boy? You still a little boy in his feelings from your Mama died, and you want to take it out on this poor, talented, young girl! You better head down to the church and right the wrongs you've been doing! Now get out my house with your drama and don't let me speak again!" I looked behind me to see Kayla already in the truck; I turned back to Uncle Frank. "Done have that girl lost with your crap! You better take care of her—whatever you have planned— because her Daddy will come and find you. He's a quiet bear, but everyone knows what he did to your Daddy and what he will do to you! Now get the fuck on before you trip on yo' damn shoes laces boy and end up hung somewhere by these fuckin' crackers who come lookin' for lost souls just like you!"

His words hit deep in my chest, and when I looked at him, his eyes changed from dark brown to grey. That's when I knew the ancestors were channeling through Uncle Frank and I had to leave, because when Uncle Frank gets like that, ain't no telling what he will do.

I turned around to look at Kayla—she was sniffing cocaine in the car. My blood started to boil, but I knew she needed this time. I took her home that day and cleaned her up. I let her sleep, fed her, and didn't leave her side. When she was strong and ready, we would begin. She needed to get in line and get her mind right…only knew one way to do that.

CHAPTER 9: DISSOCIATION

Inside? What does it look like to be inside the deep, dark caves of your fears, pain, hurts, and traumas? To be able to face the shadow of darkness that are a part of the soul? The darkness marveled inside of me, taking hold of whatever light that remained. The voice that sang to me was no longer singing. I was stuck in a fog of darkness, and all I wanted to do was numb any memory. I kept seeing Granpy's face and did everything possible to avoid his words.

I was ashamed, embarrassed, and felt hopeless. I called Daddy the moment I found out that Granpy passed, but he did not answer. I missed my Daddy, but I had a feeling he knew I was up to no good (and could not handle losing me and Mama) so, he stayed away. The silence grew louder the further my life was drifting away in the distance.

The stillness was a clouded illusion to protect me from them—an illusion that transformed what you would call reality...but what is reality when everything seems foreign anyway? What is a reality that has become so painful, you will do anything to escape it? I did not have the answers, but I could feel parts of me drifting away. I was shielding myself from anything that could kill me because the pain was that unbearable...and the only way I knew how to escape it was to numb it or hide from it by running away.

The little girl that I once knew was buried deep in a hidden part of my heart that I could no longer feel. She was buried under seventeen years of pain, abuse, neglect, trauma, and now drugs mixed with alcohol.

I stood there staring at myself in the bathroom mirror. This small, dirty ass bathroom that had not been cleaned since Uncle Andre and his hoes left for out west. I wish I went with him. He always made me feel special. The longer I sat, the more rage started to rise up through my blood veins.

"FUCK!" I paused for a moment to release some of the rage I was feeling. The bathroom mirror shattered to pieces, and my hand started bleeding immediately. Fuck, that felt good! I started licking the blood off my hand when Ice came banging on the door. Fuckin' damn annoying.

"You Girl! What's goin' on in there? Right Christ! This girl done lost her mind! OPEN THE DAMN DOOR."

His voice was getting further away in the distance. I could no longer hear Ice screaming my name. I started to see stars and my vision began to get blurry. I was looking up at the ceiling when everything faded to black.

When I woke up, everything was dark—I could not see anything. I tried to put my hand to my face but my hand was handcuffed to something. It was something metal because it made a loud bang when I pulled my hand that was locked in the handcuff, against it. I tried to move my feet but they were handcuffed too. What the fuck!

"ICE! WHERE THE FUCK ARE YOU, ICE? HELLO? HELLO?" The darkness mixed with silence was making my heart feel like it was beating outside of my chest. My breaths were short and quick. I felt like I was going into an anxiety attack.

"You goin' learn to obey! That's the problem. You haven't learned, so now I have to teach you how this works. I love you, but you must listen to me, and until you do that...you are going to stay here."

"WHAT THE FUCK ARE YOU TALKING ABOUT, ICE? You better get me the fuck..." The silence came again, but this time it was different. I felt something different in this sound of silence. It was not peaceful or relaxing. It was dark and filled with hatred. I heard a door open and some other voices were whispering to Ice, and then they all started laughing.

I heard someone say in a deep raspy voice: "I want that!"

"Just be quiet! This goin' hurt a little bit! Shhhh! My love. Shhhh!"

"ICE! What the fuck is? ICE, I CAN'T…" Ice covered my mouth with both his hands, and I could feel another man holding my legs down. A bag was put over my nose and I started breathing in large amounts of cocaine.

"You like being high, right? You like being high and not listening and making me look stupid? You like nice things, but don't like to listen or do nothing for it? That ends today. You will do what I tell you from this day forth or this is what you will deal with!"

All I could feel was my nose bleeding, and as I swallowed cocaine down my throat, my head got light and my thoughts started racing as my heart pounded faster. I wanted to speak but I could not get a word to leave my mouth. I felt the handcuffs get removed from my feet from one person, while another ripped off my panties from my body. I wanted to scream but nothing came out.

I felt someone climb on top of me and push their penis inside of me—hard. They did not say a word, and only lasted a few minutes. Another person came on top of me, and about five more after, until Ice came. I just laid there with no life in my body at that point. Ice threw a bucket of cold water on me to wake me up.

"Go fill this back up; she needs more! You Girl! Don't sleep on me. You goin' listen, right? To what Daddy tells you, right? RIGHT?" I did not respond with the last piece of defiance and self-respect I had in me. Ice slapped my face so hard it felt like my teeth were going to fly out my mouth. I could feel the blood forming in my mouth. I wanted to cry, but I was not going to give them that satisfaction. Ice punched me so hard in my face I almost passed out, and started seeing stars.

"Now I'm gonna ask you again: you're gonna listen to me and do what I say, right?" I still did respond. Then I heard a voice I recognized. I swore it was Uncle Andre.

"Uncle Andre is that you?"

"You Girl! You fuckin' high and delusional now! What the fuck, man? Imma kill this bitch. She doesn't listen!"

Ice took the handcuffs off my hands and picked me up. He lifted me as high as he could in the air and body slammed me on the hard concrete floor. I started vomiting as he kicked me in my face.

"You goin' fuckin listen! You have no family left but me, so you will do what the fuck I say. You are mine now. Do you understand?"

"She's had enough!"

"She's my girl! Don't tell me how to treat my women. You either join in, or go. You did what I asked, so we can take this game further. I did what you asked, so I can have Kayla as my girl. We even and you got what you wanted—a piece of Kayla. If you want more, you have one more shot today and then I'm leaving town, but don't ever again tell me how to treat my girl."

"You have a lot to learn about this game! Now let's get this over with." I could faintly hear the conversation, but from what I heard, it sounded like a disagreement. I started to pass out, falling asleep in agony when Ice rammed himself in my ass. I screamed so loud trying to push him off me. He started laughing and punched me in my head. He put his hand around my neck, and pushed my face into the concrete.

"My dear sweet Kayla! I saw your mother out here and she is just as miserable as she was down there. All she does is complain every day about how she has to help people she doesn't even know. How are you my sweet Kayla? My star...my sunshine. I miss you so much. I wanted to tell you that I left something for you and it's hidden in our special place. You will know when it's time to find it. It will—and I always will—keep you safe. The universe has a way of doing things, and this is all a part of the plan. You chose this just like we all did, to bring forth change, but we must break down a broken system that taught so many of us to be this way. That takes time because we have to undo what we have been programmed to believe in. Some people die without ever learning, and some spend their whole lives searching. You, my sweet Kayla, have a gift. It's buried deep inside of you, and when you choose to let the caged bird sing...you will find your way home. You will find your destiny."

"Granpy, don't go! Please, just hold me. I need you now more than ever! I'm sorry I did not get to come see you."

"Shhh! You did come see me. You have never left me. I carry a piece of you every day in my heart. You can never take that away from me. I love you."

"Lay with me, Granpy, and sing me to sleep. I'm tired."

"Shhhh! Get some rest...Granpy is here now."

The sizzling of my skin caused me to scream again in agony. I needed that to stop. It was way too much for me to handle.

"ICE, I will listen! Just stop. Fuckin' stop. I'll do whatever the fuck you want...just fuckin' stop! ICE, let me go! I said I'll listen. I'll do what you ask," I started crying uncontrollably. I couldn't stop. It was like every emotion

I had ever felt from Mama died was coming out. I heard them all laughing and the door closed.

"ICE! Take me out of here. I said I would listen! ICE! Please. I said I'll listen."

I remembered at that moment, I no longer had handcuffs on, so I ripped the blindfold off my face. It was dark, but I could see a little light underneath the gray garage door. I did not know where I was. Ice left a plastic bag beside me on the ground. When I opened it, It had a donair from mine and Daddy's favourite spot in Halifax, about five grams of cocaine, a bottle of Hennessy cognac, and some cigarettes. I was completely naked and freezing cold, and there was something burning on my lower back—I went to feel it out and screamed in agony. It felt like my skin had been burned—I felt my fingers around the lettering, and it said 'ICE.' My chest almost caved, and I started gasping for breath. He branded me like Uncle Andre branded his hoes. That meant I had to work for him—sell my body for sex. I opened the bottle of Hennessy and chugged about half of it, I ended up vomiting, and started to snort as much of a line of cocaine as I could get up my nose.

"Hold me, Granpy!"

"I'm right here, my sweet Kayla. I will always hold you!"

"Keep me warm, Granpy! I'm so cold." Granpy rocked me to sleep in his arms. I was always safe with my Granpy.

CHAPTER 10: FADED

You never really understand what it feels like to have no one, in a world full of billions. You are always on guard—always in survival mode. Your instincts heighten and you are always on alert, looking for who is out next to get you. In a sea full of sharks—trying to swim freely and not only drown or get killed—it's a skill you acquire over time. Survival of the fittest (some say) but what did I know about that? I was just a sixteen-year-old, small-figured, biracial girl from North Preston.

I had not even travelled anywhere else or experienced anything else, but I was learning real fast that I could trust no one...not even the boy I was in love with. I was starting to not recognize who he was, and just learning to accept what he wanted for us to have a good life and stop fighting him. Uncle Andre's wife did it, and they had an amazing glamorous life. She accepted her role and did as she was told.

I laid there, shivering in my thoughts, wondering how many days I was in the garage. I had no food, drink, drugs, clothes, or cigarettes. My burn must have started getting infected, because it was burning and throbbing with pain. It was starting to have little spasms. I started crying again, but what the fuck was crying going to do? Maybe I could figure out a way to get the fuck out of here and run? Run from it all, and fuck everything! Just end up in some foreign place and start a new life!

"What the fuck was that?" Footsteps were above my head. Sounded like one person. "Ice!" The garage door started to open, and then it stopped at about a quarter way up.

"Hey, You Girl! Kayla! It's your Uncle Andre. I just got back from out of town and heard what Ice's been doing to you. I can help you under one condition: you come and work for me. I will give you a job and a place to stay out of town; I can take you there now, but you have to be my girl. Uncle Andre's sweet Kayla." I wanted to vomit. I couldn't believe Uncle Andre!

"Poor chile of mine doesn't know her left foot from her right! Ain't I ever taught you anything? Listen, if you gonna survive out here now that I'm gone, you gonna have to learn how to play this game."

"Mama?"

"Just be quiet! Damn fool ain't got no sense, just like your Daddy. Good heart, but no sense. This is a trick and if you fall for it, you will pay for it twice. Do not take that man's offer. One thing about this game is two things: loyalty and respect. You can't have one without the other. If you take his offer, you done lost your loyalty with your respect, and then they know that any time someone breaks you, you will give up your loyalty. If that happens you become a bottom feeder, because ain't no one trust your ass and you end up like them hoes suckin' dick for twenty dollars. Get it together and tell that man no. Damn old fool probably can't even get it up if he wanted to."

"Kayla, You Girl! You coming or what?" I started laughing hysterically. I didn't even know why the fuck I was laughing, but it just got to that point where I couldn't do anything else but laugh.

"Uncle Andre, I knew from I was young you were fuckin' my Mama and givin' her gifts, trying to get me. I was the one you always wanted, but see...I already have my Daddy, and his name is Ice! The only Daddy for me. You got my Mama—you could never have me. Now get the fuck on, and go find your other hoes!"

"Now I see why Ice beats your ass! But one thing I won't deny is...you are solid, and if you are smart, you will go very far. I saw it in you from a kid. You have a different spirit. You can light the magic in any room and not every woman has that gift. Some just have pussy, but no magic. You have it all! Goodbye, Kayla. Oh...one more thing. Your Daddy asked me to give this to you. It was his last words before I...nevermind." He started laughing and threw Daddy's chain he always wore at me—it had a locket with a photo of Mama and me in it. He always told me that if he died, that it would find its way to me.

"WHAT THE FUCK DID YOU DO?" I ran to attack the garage door when he shut it closed.

"I gave my son what he asked for: you." I fell to the concrete pavement, lifeless. Everything I had left in me was gone. I had no one. I had no breath. I had no more fight left in me. I laid there sobbing in a puddle of my own blood, mixed with tears. I held Daddy's chain in my hand...the only piece of him I had left.

"DADDY! DADDY!"

The garage opened and Ice picked me off the ground.

"Shhh! It's ok, baby. Daddy's here now!" He kissed me all over my face while wiping my tears away, and put me inside the backseat of his truck.

"It's all gonna be ok. You're with your Daddy now. I'm going to clean you up. I got you a whole bunch of gifts and stuff. I love you baby! Just listen to me now, so we don't have to go through this again. Ok?"

"Yes, Daddy."

"That's my good baby. Now get some rest. We are almost home."

The smell of something sweet cooking in the kitchen was like magic to my soul; I was so grateful for the mornings I got up to Mama's cooking. I could hear her yelling at Daddy.

"Get your fingers out the pot and wait for it to be done!"

Daddy would laugh and kiss Mama to make her smile. Mama would feed him some more before everyone sat down to eat. It was their love language. Daddy would feed Mama's ego and allow her to feel special. In return, Mama would fulfill Daddy's needs to keep him happy and committed.

I opened my eyes to smell of Mama's cooking, but as I looked around the room, this was far from home with Daddy and Mama. Tears filled my eyes immediately once I realized both my parents were dead. My Granpy died. All I had now was Ice—he was my only family left.

I started looking around at the room that was unfamiliar; I was in a big king size bed that could swallow me whole, with couture gold and black Versace sheets. The pillows were big and fluffy and half the size of my body. Where the fuck was I? I sat up for a second, but my head was banging with a headache, so I had to lay back down right quick. I noticed as I was about to lay down there were rose petals on the floor. Where the fuck was Ice, and what the fuck was going on?

I reached for my neck to feel the bruises and if this was really real or just a dream. I felt a chain around my neck—it was Daddy's pendant. I held it so close to my chest while the anger filled with hurt riddled my body. I could not believe Uncle Andre would do that to his own cousin! What did Daddy do to offend him? I had so many questions. My mind was running in so many different directions. I just wanted it all to stop.

"STOP!" Ice walked in the room with a tray of food that smelled delicious, and a big smile on his face that I did not return. He was cleaned up in his best clothing and had on some cologne that smelled so good.

"Hi, my baby! Did you just wake up?" I did not answer. I just kept looking at him.

"It's ok, you don't gotta say anything right now. I know it's been a lot. We went through a lot." Did this muthafucka say 'we,' because I didn't remember 'us' going through anything! I remembered 'me' dealing with all this shit alone. His words began to sound like a foreign language I could not understand.

"Kayla? You hear me? Kayla?" The chills that came over my body. I wanted to scream, but the sounds would not come out.

"You get more bees with honey, damn fool! Show that boy you can be what he needs, and he will give you what you want!" Mama and her damn bees with honey crap!

"Would you stop? Ain't no damn bees…"

"Kayla? You ok, baby?"

"Yeah. I'm really tired and hungry. How long have I been asleep?"

"'Bout a week or so, but on and off. You needed the rest and to nourish your body. We have lots of work ahead. We are leaving in two days to head to Toronto."

"TORONTO? For what?"

"I just told you, baby, we have work to do but don't worry about that right now. Let me take care of my baby. Eat this breakfast; I drove down to Cora's in Dartmouth because I know you love their breakfast, so I ordered eggs benedict, fruit, sausage, bacon, and OJ. We gotta leave soon also, because they sayin' something about a virus in China or some shit. I don't know what that means, but the whole country got locked down—they are saying it's killing people off or some shit."

"How the fuck do you know, and since when did you start watching the news? Isn't that your Daddy?"

"Daddy told me it's gonna happen in the year twenty twenty. That's next year, Kayla. He said it's some plandemic shit for them to plant us with microchips—

some toxic virus to make money off us like lab rats and force the world into the last phase of the New World Order."

"Ice, stay off the drugs! You and your crazy Daddy talking crap! Look, if this is gonna work and you're gonna be my Daddy, don't you ever bring up the muthafucka that killed my Daddy, and fed my Mama the drugs that killed her. You understand me? You're my Daddy now. If we are gonna do this together because you love me and I love you, that nigga is dead to you now. Do you understand me?"

" I got you, baby!" Ice leaned over and kissed me on my lips, so soft and gentle. He started spoon feeding me my breakfast; he kept smiling from ear to ear, grilling his mouth full of gold grills, and I wanted to melt. He looked good. I would do anything for him, but a part of me also feared him because I knew what he could do to me when he was angry.

"Ya, that's my baby! Being a good girl for her Daddy." Ice continued feeding me until the food was finished, and then passed me my glass of orange juice from the wooden breakfast tray. I wanted to ask him where he had taken me, but too many questions always got Ice angry. He was being so loving to me now…if only we could stay here. If only it could just be Ice and I building our own life. I wished he could love me how my Daddy loved my Mama.

"Baby? Are you there? I bought you some nice things I thought you would like. Maybe you could take a nice bubble bath with me and try 'em on after?"

"Ok baby…on one condition?"

"What?"

"Can you get us some drinks and some MDMA?"

"I got all that for you and more, baby love!"

"I told your stupid ass you could get more bees with honey! 'Bout time you start listening to your Mama, 'cause your Daddy and Granpy ain't got no damn sense. Always get taken for damn fools, and you gonna be next thinking anyone out here loves you more than you need to. People only love themselves and what they can get from you."

"MAMA! Shut the fuck UP!"

"What you say, You Girl? Who you talkin' to out here?"

"Nobody, baby. Is the bath ready yet?"

"Yes, baby! I got the music, champagne, and all the party favours you need. All you gotta do is slide right on in. You coming?" Ice reached out his hand, but I needed a moment.

"I'm coming, baby! Just give me a second—I'll be in there soon."

"Oh! Baby, there's a tray right there in front of the mirror by the bed. I put some Scoobie snacks on there for ya." Ice walked out the room in his white and gold Versace robe and slippers—he was highly dressed for this occasion. I needed something to get my mood right because my head was lost, and God knew I ain't know where to find it.

I stood in front of the mirror, looking deep into my eyes (that used to be full of light, but had turned dark and soulless). The little girl that was full of song mixed with joy was nowhere to be found.

The tray Ice left on the table in front of the glass mirror by the bed had a bag of cocaine with a crisp one-hundred-dollar bill on it. I made the biggest line I could across that tray and snorted as much as I could up my nose before making my way to my Daddy Ice.

CHAPTER 11: CRUSH

The drive from Downtown Halifax to Toronto took us almost a full twenty-four hours. We made a few stops along the way. I realized after leaving the spot we were staying at that Ice rented a luxury Airbnb mansion (that his Daddy or his Daddy's wife must have got from a client, because I doubt he found that shit himself). The spot was in Dartmouth—which was not far from Halifax—but Ice had to pick up something downtown, so I made sure to grab a donair from the Tony's on Robie Street before we jumped on highway 2BW for Toronto.

My nerves were shot the fuck up. I mean, I never left Nova Scotia, and I was not sure what the fuck I was going to be doing in some big city with six million people.

I had to admit, I slept a lot of the ride to clear my mind and try to prepare for what was next—there was way too much bullshit in my head from my life in North Preston, and this was a way to forget it all. I mean, why not make fuckin' money and have a life with my baby? What the fuck was back there for me in North Preston, but Ice's Daddy trying to get me to be one of his hoes? It was not gonna happen.

Mama would be rolling ten times over in her grave if I let that nigga be my Daddy. Granpy was gone, and any chance of me believing I was going to be a singer like Granpy died with him when he passed away. That little girl no longer existed—she died with each and every one of them. The only thing left was a distant memory of all the people who were so broken (from a system that was built to make them fail), but at the same time...they had a deep love for each other and their community. Like family.

You can't teach love when it's never taught to you. You can't love if you don't know love. History always has a way of coming back around.

When we arrived in downtown Toronto, the first thing I noticed was the smell and the mass amount of people. It had a completely different smell than North Preston: it stunk like sewage, and the streets were flooded with people everywhere. I mean, you saw all different types of races: Black, white, Indian...fuck! They had the whole damn rainbow in them streets. The buildings were so tall and everything was so compact. I felt like I was getting swallowed whole at one point. It was like being a kid and looking up at how big everything was. That's how I felt.

"Gimme a minute; I'll be right back? Imma just check us into this spot right here."

"Wait! Where you goin'? You can't leave me in these streets all by myself! Are you crazy, Ice? I don't even know where the fuck I'm at." This nigga was always trying some bullshit. How the fuck you bring me to a new city and leave me in the fuckin' car by my damn self? Like, he was always on some bullshit.

"Look, You Girl, just wait. Right Christ! Always gotta be gettin' on my damn nerves." Ice left the car with his keys and locked the doors. My blood started to boil.

"Sugar with honey, Chile!"

"Woman, I told you that ain't the advice she needs. Stop givin' her your bullshit advice because it's only gonna get her dead or in jail!"

"DADDY? Is that you? DADDY? DADDY?"

"The whole fuckin' street don't need to know I'm your Daddy, Kayla! Fuck, man! I seriously wish you would just shut the fuck up 'cause I'm gettin' pissed the fuck off now. JUST SHUT THE FUCK UP!" Ice slammed my head against the passenger side window and pushed my face so hard into the glass, my front teeth felt like they were going to shatter the window.

"Ice, please!" I said clawing his arm, begging for him to stop when he slapped me across my face.

"SHUT THE FUCK UP! Get your fuckin' dumb hoe ass out the car and do what the fuck I tell you. I don't want to hear you speak until I ask you to speak, do you understand me?"

"Ye..." He grabbed my head with his hands and slammed it on the dashboard of the passenger side of the car. I started seeing stars again, and my eyes got blurry.

"Check that fuckin' mouthpiece of yours and close your fuckin' mouth! DO YOU UNDERSTAND ME?" Even if I could speak, I was not goin' to bother at that point.

"I told you stop listenin' to your dumb ass Daddy. He doesn't know shit about shit!" I hated when Mama was right, but the more I used my heart, the more I would get burned.

I loved Andre Junior, and a part of me would always love that boy. Ice survived when Andre Junior could not. Kayla was gone, so who the fuck did that leave me to be?

"Let's go. Take this and clean up your face! I got someone comin' by the hotel to help you with make-up and outfits." Ice walked around to the passenger side of the car and yanked me out with no mercy. I pulled my black Chanel hood over my head, and put on my all-black Chanel glasses with the all-white Chanel logo on the side. I looked down on the ground and kept my head buried in my hood as much as possible while I wiped the blood from my lip, and the tears from my eyes.

I was sick and fuckin' tired of lettin' this nigga see me down on my face like a little bitch. He really thought this shit was about him. He didn't fuckin' realize I had nothing left, so it didn't matter what the fuck I felt, or what this dumb ass nigga did. I lost all emotions and feelings for anyone or anything—I was just fuckin' surviving.

The Courtyard Marriott was located downtown Toronto, right by the Eaton Centre. It was the middle of the city, and the main attraction to the livelihood of the downtown core—everything was just a step away. The hotel itself had a restaurant and a gym, but of course Ice made it clear upon arrival that I would not be able to leave my room unless he said so.

As we walked in the hotel and Ice led the way through reception, I was mesmerized at how fancy the hotel was, and by all the traffic: all the classy professional businessmen coming in and out of the hotel with their work bags. This shit smelled like money! I mean, no wonder Ice chose this spot. He was always good at finding the money, like he dreamt about the shit in his sleep. It was the only time he was quiet (or when he was getting some good head).

Our room was on the twenty-third floor, room three thirty-three.

"Get your ass in the shower and clean yourself up. I'll bring some shavers with all that stuff we bought before we left. You have to clean yourself before you get to work. We tryna bring in a few customers for the first couple nights that we are here, so clean up, my cousin. Shenell gonna be here when you come out: she's gonna do your hair and makeup. Then she's gonna get you in some nice gear and one of them online ads so we can start working together, baby Kayla. When you start working, what do you want your working name to be? You can talk now." His smile was so big, I could see all his gold teeth shining from ear to ear. His light skin was shining like he just took a fresh shower, and his skin was melting with cocoa butter. He was so fine with all his gold jewelry, but such a bad boy at heart.

"Ok Junior, my Daddy! I think something like Pocahontas would be ok, but what do you think? It's always what my Daddy says, baby."

"You ain't called me that in a long time."

"Is that ok, Daddy?"

"Ya, but I prefer Daddy because that's who I am: your king. So Pocahontas is ok. Is she going to do whatever I need and say? She's gonna work hard to build our family, so we can leave this game and have our kids? She's gonna serve Daddy and be Daddy's wife, so we can be like Jay-Z and Beyonce?"

"Yes, my Daddy!"

"Then forget about Kayla and Andre Junior—we left them back home. Now go clean up because Shenell goin' be up here right quick and I want us to get to work. I have another room down the hall; once y'all ready, I'm going to set up shop. So don't have me wait too long."

I began to explore the possibility that the more I got into my new work position, it might not be as bad as I thought. I entered the washroom, and there was a bag of cocaine on the counter, with one pill of MDMA. The numbness was my way to cope and get the money for us to get out.

"Now you are understanding. Smart cookie. I knew it wouldn't take you that long to get it. You have to realize—you have my blood in your genes. The Scottish blood, and we are warriors of conquering pain. Battles won and many deaths within us...and you have that in your blood. No one—or nothing—will defeat you, but yourself. Just like no one defeated me but myself, Kayla. The choice is always yours."

I rolled the crisp hundred-dollar bill Ice left on a metal tray that was laced with a bag of cocaine on the marble sink bathroom countertop. I made myself an average line (because I knew it was just a pick-me-up) so I could not feel too much, but also so I was still capable enough to function...or else there would have been a bottle to go with it. I turned the hot water on in the clean, nice, spacious, all-white bathroom, and hopped in the shower. I started singing the song that I recorded with Uncle Frank, and tears started to fill my eyes.

> *Take me away from this place,*
> *I never belonged here anyway...*
> *My Mama is gone*
> *My Daddy is Daddy dead*
> *My Mama OD on heroin*
> *Just take me away from this place...*
> *Just please, please...*

I sat at the bottom of that tub and let the hot water fall down on my naked bruised face and my tears until I could no longer hear Kayla sing that song deep inside of me. I buried all that was left of music and song in that moment, in that bathtub.

CHAPTER 12: TELLY T

Shenell must have been in the streets for years because her face had scars that told many stories, just like her dark, brown, cold eyes. She had long, golden, curly hair that was pulled back in a ponytail. Her dark bags around her eyes made her always look like she was tired from lack of sleep. She had a teardrop tattoo on the right side of her face, below her eye—I wondered if it had the same meaning that most teardrop tattoos did. I wondered if she was a killer in her past and had taken a life.

    She was short like Mama—not taller than five feet—and had a big ass (you could not help but look at). She was dressed in a one-piece jumper with Louis Vuitton sneakers and a purse to match. Her hair was dyed bleach blonde and she had a stack of jewelry on. She looked at me like I was a doll or something she was going to play with—she definitely did not look at me as a human being. I sat on the bed in my bra and panties, silently waiting for direction while her and Ice spoke briefly before Ice exited the room, leaving her with a cell phone.

"How was the trip up here from down home?" she asked, not looking in my face, but scanning my body while directing me with her hand to stand up and turn around. She rustled through a bag on the floor and grabbed some lingerie pieces for me to try on. I did as I was told without a word, remembering Ice's words about making money and getting straight to work.

Shenell liked the first lingerie outfit I put on—it was an all-black laced up one piece with leather straps to hold it together. It was sexy, and I started to feel a part of myself emerging that I never felt before. I felt like a grown woman who could take control of any situation if I played my cards right. I smiled at myself in the mirror beside the bed.

"Yeessssssssssss! You Girl! That's the look right there! They are goin' to love you. You are going to make a killin' out here in these streets. Take that hair down and make it wild with all them dark curly curls. I brought some light green contacts to give you an even sexier look. You should try 'em. Ice told me we are going with Pocahontas as the name. Why did you choose that name?"

"I just liked the movie when I was growing up."

"That's funny, because she was an Indigenous woman that saved many European colonizers from dying by the hands of her family and tribe. She later got convinced to marry the Europeans and was forced to become Christian and get rid of her name. She changed it to Rebecca Wolfe. It's a very interesting story about how the European colonizers did the same thing here in Canada. They did it to Black and Indigenous people of colour. They wonder why we have fought so hard to survive, you know?" I nodded my head, but I clearly had no clue what she was talking about. I thought Pocahontas was just a cartoon character that I was in love with because she was so cute and pretty. I figured I could be sexy like her and get lost in my work…leaving whatever was behind me.

"Let's get these pictures so we can get the ad up and running, and then we can get to work. Scared money don't make no money, and we can't sleep on shit. Hop on the bed over there and get on your knees with your ass up in the air. I don't want to see your face, just your ass." I admit, I was very uncomfortable, but I did as I was told. I could see Daddy and Granpy with such disappointment in their eyes and hearts.

"Can you give me a second? I just need the bathroom right quick." Shenell nodded in annoyance but rushed me quickly to the bathroom. I needed a line to get my mind and body right. I quickly grabbed a big bump and got myself ready to get back to work.

"You ready now?"

"Yes. Let's get to it?" I jumped on the bed as I could taste the cocaine taste dripping down my throat. I got a feeling of sexual seductiveness mixed with sensuality and I was in the mood to be Pocahontas. I was bringing her alive with each breath and each moment; she was me, and I was her.

"There's something different about you! You are not like these other hoes. You have something special about you. Once you start, you will know how to do many things other women can't. You will be a natural at this game!" I could hear Uncle Andre's voice; as I took each photo, the more empowered and sexual I felt. The more I started to take control of the bed and the camera, the more empowered I became.

"Easy! We ain't even got to work yet, but I can see you are ready. Have you worked before?"

"No," I said quietly.

"Look, ain't no shame in the game. If you don't get it, someone else will. I was in this game for years in my time. I made a killing, and you can do the same. I'm going to give you one tip and don't ever tell anyone I told you: pussy is power, and if you know how to use your pussy for power, you will control any situation you are in. Also, if you know how to use your pussy to get money...you have won the game, and will always be in control."

I listened to Shenell's wise words and promised myself to never forget them. I sat at the edge of the bed with my legs crossed, and for the first time in a while, a smile appeared on my face. I started laughing and Shenell looked at me like I was crazy.

"You one of those ones, huh? You're gonna do just fine! The ads are gonna be up in thirty minutes; I'm going to go see Ice and let him know we are ready. Do you want to eat some food and have a bit of a drink before we get to work?"

"A drink would be good. Calm my nerves a bit," I mumbled.

"I can't hear you! Cat must have got your damn tongue. Look, I'll get you some food and a little drink to relax you, but not to get you sloppy because that's how you lose money. Get your mind and body in order. Spray some perfume for the first client that will be coming. Oh, before I forget...when the client comes to the door, always make sure anything you have valuable is either locked in the safe or put away. You always look through the peephole before you open the door because it could be fuckin' undercovers actin' like they are clients, or Ice, or hotel services. Always look first. Third thing: before anything goes down, the first thing that should happen is that the client puts the money on the dresser. We will text you a number, and that will be the amount. Make sure you count it and DON'T do anything before you collect, count, and put the money away. Now for full sex—always with a condom—it's one thousand for thirty minutes. These are not the regular rates. We are charging this high (and can) because you are younger, so they will pay for more. Do not take less than what we tell you. Do not do more than what we tell you, and don't ever go over your time unless they are willing to pay more upfront and you have the money in your hand and let us know. Do you understand?" I nodded, and did not say a word.

"You are very quiet. Are you ok?"

"Yes. Just want to get to work. That's what I'm here for."

"Ok. Ok. Say less, ma."

The knock at the door sent chills down my body. I was ready, but nervous as hell. I chugged down the drink of rum and Coke that I just made, while shoving a piece of Popeye's fried chicken in my mouth. I ran to the bathroom and checked to see if I looked ok, and quickly chugged some Listerine around my mouth so my breath did not smell like fried chicken and rum.

There was another knock at the door, but it was gentle. I looked through the peephole and saw a short Asian man with glasses. This had to be him.

I slowly unlocked and opened the door.

"Hi."

"Pocha..."

"Shhhh. Come inside." I looked quickly outside to see if anyone else was around, but saw no one. The short man was already inside and he smelled like ramen noodles mixed with cigarette smoke. He took his shoes off and he had no socks on: first turn off. Who does not wear socks with shoes?

"You do blow job and sex? Fifteen hundred for one hour?"

"Excuse me, it's two grand an hour, and that does not include blow jobs—that's more, and condoms only."

"Ok. Ok. You play hard for such a new baby. I never seen you before, and you pretty."

"Do you have it or not? Please don't waste my time. Put the money on the table." He walked over to the table and counted out a bunch of hundred-dollar bills, then he looked at me, and then down at my feet, before dropping to the ground.

"Oh my! Pretty feet! I love pretty feet. I don't want sex. I just want to lay here, talk, and look at your toes. Can I touch them?" Was this fuckin' boy serious? Who pays two grand to stare at feet?

"Yes. Just give me a minute. I need to use the bathroom." I needed a drink for this bullshit. I wanted to laugh, but heard some rustling in the other room. When I came out, the dude was naked in my lingerie, dancing in the mirror.

"You ever try cocaine, Pocha?"

"Yes."

"Oh, good girl. I bring so we can have fun." This couldn't be as bad as I thought.

CHAPTER 13: CLOCKS

"You fuckin' dumb bitch! Suck it fuckin' harder, you slut! HARDER!" His strong, thick, dark Black hands wrapped around my neck and I started to claw at his arms. He started laughing in my face when he threw me down on the bed. He ripped my panties off and tried to shove his big Black penis inside me, but I kicked him as hard as I could. I somehow wiggled my way out of his grip and tried to run for the door to go get Ice, when something hit me so hard over the head...I saw stars. I collapsed to the floor and tried clawing at the carpet to the front door.

He yanked me so hard off the ground, and back to the bed. I started screaming as loud as I could because I knew this sick fuckin' monster of a man was going to rape me. I should have known that! He came into the room looking like he was a saint in some business suit, but his hair was not combed, and his glasses looked like they were years old. His nails were full of dirt and his dick smelled like it had not been washed in weeks. Something was different about this dude...and I felt it when he entered the room.

He had a problem with paying first, and from there it went downhill. I texted Ice and Shenell to tell them something was not right about this nigga, but I got no fuckin' response. I had pepper spray, but my fuckin' purse was in the washroom.

"I know just the type of trash you are. Think you special 'cause you light-skin and pretty? I enjoy breakin' hoes like you down. It's what I do...and take all your fuckin' money." I started to scream again when he slapped me so hard in my face that I could not see, and my ears started ringing.

"Silence is the only way to handle monsters like this. You don't fight back or anything...you just let them take what they want."

"Don't listen to him. This why your Uncle Andre killed his ass, because he just lays down like a fuckin' dog to his master. Listen to me: there is a pen on the other side of you that dropped out of his pocket. Grab the pen and stab him as hard as you can. If you want to kill him: in his neck right below his chin...and if you don't: stab him right in the eye or cheek, but you have to fast, Pocha, because you don't have time. He will kill you."

"I can't!"

"Kayla, shut-up!"

"But Granpy..."

"Oh, Granpy, Granpy! Pocha, do what I said, or this man is goin' to kill you."

•

"Fuckin' goof ass nigga, man. I already told you, Shenell, don't send her no niggas, man! I step away for fuckin' one hour, and look at this fuckin' mess I had to come back to and fix! If Pocha didn't stab this muthafucka, she'd be dead. Yo, go call Bubba. Tell him come here and come clean this mess up man before the fuckin' cleaner gets here."

"Nigga acted..."

"How long you been in the game? Actually, don't even answer that. This happens again, everybody gonna pay."

"Nigga, calm down!"

"Calm! She could have been dead...then what?"

"Many hoes have died out here; she wouldn't have been the first."

"GET THE FUCK OUT, AND GO GET FUCKIN' BUBBA!"

I was laying in the bed while Ice cleaned me up; I felt his hurt and anger all over the room. It was filling the walls with all of his energy. Tears just kept rolling down my face.

"Look. Shit like this does happen—and I'm not going to say it doesn't—but we are always prepared for anything, like our people have always been. By any means necessary. That pig of a man ain't no man. He's lookin' for anyone to take advantage of, for his sad life. That's why I did what I did to him. I won't let that happen to you again, and from now on I'll make sure you're always protected." I looked at Ice deep in his eyes to see if there was any truth to what he was telling me. I was not sure who to trust at that point. What if it was another test to break me down and see what I could handle, or how I would react? There was a quick knock at the door.

"No more today. Ice, please. I need a break."

"It's ok. It's just Bubba. Remember Bubba from down home? He's just here to clean up the mess; he won't harm you. I'll be back. I have to deal with Shenell." I grabbed the pocketknife from underneath the pillow; it was always there in case I had any problems, but I never expected this. This was beyond horrific.

Ice opened the door and a big, tall, dark-skinned man walked in; his hair was long and braided, and he had sunglasses on and a hood over his head. He was in all black with big workman's boots. He said something briefly to Ice, and then Ice left the hotel suite. I started looking at him, but he did not look back. Instead, he put his headphones on and pulled some stuff from his bag: big black garbage bags, scissors, duct tape, bleach, and some next spray bottle.

"I only be a minute, ma'am!" He was acting like a bigger version of Bubba, but something was wrong…like he was slow or something. He started humming, and got on the ground to clean up the mess from Ice and I.

"Take me away from the place; I never belonged anyway." My heart sank into my chest, and tears filled my eyes. With all the pain…I did not care.

I jumped up off the bed, limping, and touched Bubba on his back. He jumped because he did not see me and did not expect me to touch him.

"Where did you hear that song you are singing?"

"A friend of mine from back home, Kayla, made it, and now everyone all over the radio is playing it. Our Uncle Frank had a producer come by and he heard the song while Uncle Frank was playing it…and he sent it to his friends on the radio. Now it's a big hit, but it's sad because Kayla is missing, and everyone thinks she's dead like her parents. Sad story, but that shit happens in life, you know." The front door to the hotel opened, and I jumped back in the bed. Ice came walking in the door.

"You almost done, nigga? We ain't got all day, and Pochahontas gots to get back to work. We have more money to make, and you know how I get when there's money to be made, Bubba!"

"Yes, boss. I'll cut your hair in a minute. I was just telling her about Kayla, the girl we knew…"

"What did I tell you 'bout talkin' to the women? My nigga, don't talk to 'em unless I tell you to. Now get back to work…I have another job for you." Ice looked at me to see if anything—or any emotion—was coming from me, but I just closed my eyes to act like I was falling asleep. I felt him walk towards the bed and run his hand across my forehead.

"Everything will be ok. You are the love of my life. We will make it to the top together. Just trust me and let me show you the way to the top, baby. You are the only one that is built for this game like me."

I remained silent as I felt another part of my heart die that day—another part I knew would never come back. Ice was right about one thing: I was the only one that was built for this game just like him. I guess Mama was right...it was in my blood. It was a part of her that she passed down to me, and a part of me that I could never get rid of. A part of me that kept me surviving. A part of me that kept me going. A part of me that knew I could rise in this game. Ice was right. I saw his vision and knew my role.

Kamilah Haywood

Kamilah Haywood

Kamilah Haywood

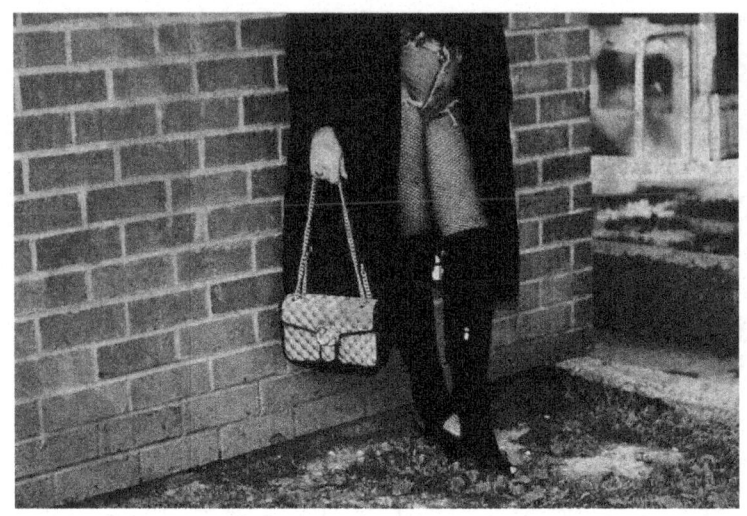

AUTHOR'S WORDS

This is not a dedication: these are just some last-minute thoughts about this book, why I decided to write this piece, and why I decided to work with the amazing team of women that I chose, who immaculately executed this piece with me and my vision that I had for it.

This book is not to put down or demonize the "pimp" or the "victim." In this story, there are many victims of a broken system that has been imposed on the minority (who is clearly the majority) for decades. There has been a dark system preying on the minds of the masses and subjecting us to oppression, systemic racism, genocides, economic starvation, poverty, and a lack of educational truth and historical facts.

When you live in a system and you are the hunted—the prey, the oppressed, the broken, the consumer, the lab rat, the products and the programmed of the Black Indigenous People of Colour, the Women, the Outliers, 2LGBTQ+—the answer will always be death.

Death of the mind...death of the body...but they can NEVER take the spirit/soul. We are all connected on the universal order of the Hidden Track by universal LAW. All is one and one is all. You can only control the masses with dark, evil energy for so many decades before the universe makes you reap what you sow.

To all those voices who have been silenced, lost, and forgotten...or who died without anyone even knowing...they thought hunting people as prey (not realizing you are turning them into predators) would one day backfire in the end.

Universal law at its finest. To be continued...

Thank you.

K. Haywood

Made in the USA
Monee, IL
02 December 2021